Bullshit, Backlash & Bleeding Hearts

David Slack is a speechwriter and columnist who has written speeches for a number of New Zealand politicians since 1989. A graduate in law from Victoria University, he has worked in advertising and public relations. His website www.speeches.com, which enables users to generate speeches automatically, has an international clientele. His columns appear on the popular New Zealand web log www.PublicAddress.Net. He lives in Devonport with his wife and daughter.

bullshit, backlash & bleeding hearts

A confused person's guide to The Great Race Row

DAVID SLACK

PENGUIN BOOKS

PENGUIN BOOKS
Published by the Penguin Group
Penguin Group (NZ), cnr Airborne and Rosedale Roads, Albany,
Auckland 1310, New Zealand
Penguin Books Ltd, 80 Strand, London, WC2R 0RL, England
Penguin Group (USA) Inc., 375 Hudson Street, New York, NY 10014, United States
Penguin Group (Australia), 250 Camberwell Road, Camberwell,
Victoria 3124, Australia
Penguin Books Canada Ltd, 10 Alcorn Avenue, Toronto,
Ontario, Canada M4V 3B2
Penguin Books (South Africa) (Pty) Ltd, 24 Sturdee Avenue, Rosebank,
Johannesburg 2196, South Africa
Penguin Books India (P) Ltd, 11, Community Centre, Panchsheel Park,
New Delhi 110 017, India
Penguin Ireland Ltd, 25 St Stephen's Green, Dublin 2, Ireland
Penguin Books Ltd, Registered Offices: 80 Strand, London, WC2R 0RL, England

First published by Penguin Group (NZ), 2004
3 5 7 9 10 8 6 4 2

Designed by Mary Egan
Typeset by Egan-Reid Ltd
Printed in Australia by McPherson's Printing Group

ISBN 0 14 301952 X
A catalogue record for this book is available
from the National Library of New Zealand.

www.penguin.co.nz

Contents

	Preface	7
	Introduction	11
Chapter One	**The new 'separatism'**	19
Chapter Two	**Arrival times**	25
Chapter Three	**The gamble**	33
Chapter Four	**Bad faith**	45
Chapter Five	**'A dying race'**	65
Chapter Six	**Resistance**	73
Chapter Seven	**Back to the future**	83
Chapter Eight	**Partners in time**	95
Chapter Nine	**Early settlement**	107
Chapter Ten	**Money justice**	117
Chapter Eleven	**The principle issue**	129
Chapter Twelve	**The 'gravy train'**	135
Chapter Thirteen	**Preference and privilege**	143
Chapter Fourteen	**Culture gap**	147
Chapter Fifteen	**The co-op solution**	157
Chapter Sixteen	**Lines in the sand**	165
Chapter Seventeen	**The good news**	173
Chapter Eighteen	**Conclusion**	183
	Bibliography	197
	Quiz answers	199

For Mary-Margaret

Preface

THIS IS really a book for my generation and my parents' generation – we're the ones who came late to this story. We're familiar with fragments of our history and we know a thing or two about the Treaty of Waitangi, but we don't often know it with great certainty. For every fact or opinion you go to offer at a dinner party, it seems there's someone ready with a contradiction. Who's right? The idea of this book is to help settle a few of those arguments by filling in the gaps in the jigsaw – who did what and when, who's complaining and why, who's right, who's wrong, who's mistaken and who's just making trouble.

I learned a little about the Treaty in law school, and I learned a good deal more as a speechwriter in the Beehive. Although I'm no expert, I'm familiar with, if you like, the scene of the crime. I've worked with a number of the people who have had important roles in the story. You'll hear from them – as well as a number of other authorities and important players – throughout this book. My role here really is to be your guide, to ask the questions on your behalf. Many of my sources need little introduction, but for the sake of completeness some brief descriptions may be helpful.

Sir Geoffrey Palmer was Minister of Justice, Attorney-General, Deputy Prime Minister and Prime Minister in the Labour administration that effectively put the Treaty back into play. Sir Douglas Graham was Minister of Justice and Minister in Charge of Treaty of Waitangi Negotiations in the National administration that reached the major historic settlements over the fisheries, Tainui and Ngai Tahu claims.

Alex Frame is a Wellington barrister and academic. As founding director of the Treaty of Waitangi Policy Unit in the Department of Justice, he played an important role in helping the Government formulate Treaty policy in the late 1980s. He has been a teacher of public law for many years, and has advised extensively on Treaty matters in New Zealand.

Professor Matthew Palmer is Dean of Law at Victoria University. He was Crown Negotiator for the Treasury in the first historical Treaty settlement, and played a significant role in helping the government develop policies for settling Treaty claims.

Tom Bennion is a Wellington barrister with many years' experience in the Waitangi Tribunal. As editor of the *Maori Law Review* he is a keen observer and insightful analyst of the evolving Treaty story.

Sir Tipene O'Regan is a Ngai Tahu kaumatua. He chaired the Treaty of Waitangi Fisheries Commission, the Sealord Group of companies and the Ngai Tahu Maori Trust Board. He led the Ngai Tahu land and sea fisheries claims before the Waitangi Tribunal, played a central role in the Treaty fisheries settlements and led the Ngai Tahu Claim settlement negotiations.

Shane Jones is chairman of Te Ohu Kai Moana (the Treaty

of Waitangi Fisheries Commission).

Moana Maniapoto, who as a performer and composer is taking Maori culture around the world, has also been involved in many aspects of the contemporary debate, as an advocate for the Maori voice in various official bodies and as an occasional media commentator.

Dame Anne Salmond, Professor and Pro-Vice-Chancellor at the University of Auckland, is one of New Zealand's most prominent anthropologists and historians.

I interviewed a number of ministers in the current administration: Michael Cullen is Deputy Prime Minister and Minister of Finance; Margaret Wilson's portfolios include Minister of Justice and Minister in Charge of Treaty of Waitangi Negotiations; John Tamihere's responsibilities include Associate Minister of Maori Affairs. Don Brash, of course, leads the National Party and would like to lead a government.

Finally, Ranginui Walker was good enough to share forthcoming chapters of a new edition of his *Ka Whawhai Tonu Matou – Struggle without End*. I am most grateful for the insights he offered, and to all my sources for their time and knowledge.

We'll be hearing from all of these participants at various points in the story. We'll also be considering the perspective of the stereotypical angry talkback caller from time to time – the chapter titles have been given over to them to have their say. After all, it's not a real debate if you're not hearing all sides of the argument, is it?

For a debate to be worthwhile, we need to know what it is we're arguing about. This is not an exhaustive treatment of the topic, but it will arm you with enough information to make your case the next time this comes up over a bottle or two. If we all end up a little better informed, that will do this debate no harm at all.

TEST YOUR TREATY KNOWLEDGE 1

What has been the approximate total cost of Treaty of Waitangi settlements since 1989?

- **A. $481 million**
- **B. $596 million**
- **C. $709 million**
- **D. $1.23 billion**
- **E. $2.51 billion**

(Answers page 199)

Introduction

DOES THIS ever happen to you on your Christmas holidays? You're all sitting around having a beer, someone's turning the meat on the barbecue, the sun's sinking below the hills, and the worries of the frantic last-minute December rush are all disappearing. You can't help it; you all start talking about politics.

You can happily let months go by without swapping thoughts with friends and family about the things the Government is doing, but now you're in the mood to open up. The results can sometimes surprise you.

Didn't think he'd be feeling that upset about it.

Must remember not to ask her that again.

And you can surprise yourself.

Did I just say that?

Where it gets especially interesting is when people get the chance to say the things they normally keep to themselves.

I know this isn't very PC but ...

Or they feel able to speak freely among friends.

I tell you what really makes me sick ...

So what did you talk about over your 2003 Christmas holidays? The Treaty of Waitangi perhaps? If you did, you weren't alone. I heard a few things from some unexpected quarters that startled me:

Fed up ... Gone far enough.

A politician with an eye to the polls will sometimes spot an opportunity in this. We don't know exactly what Don Brash did for his Christmas holidays, but we do know that he spent some time getting ready for a speech.

I've had a little to do with this process myself as a political speechwriter. Politicians want to start the new year with as much noise as they can. They prepare a weighty piece that pronounces on the state of the nation, or words to that effect, and they try to stake out the battleground. They're all very keen, a little like a class of eager six-year-olds: *Pick me, pick me!*

Don Brash had a particular need to be picked. He'd not long taken over the leadership of the National Party, which job he'd been handed in the not un-pressured context that the party needed to lift its polling off the mat.

The Orewa Rotary Club has had a long tradition of affording a prominent politician that opportunity to pronounce. Such speeches can be a little daunting at the blank-page stage. There's plenty to talk about – too much. You have to decide what's most important to the audience and give it a good push. Like all political speeches, you're also writing for two audiences – the good people who have made the effort to come, sit and listen to you; and the fickle people out in TV, radio and newspaper land who may or may not spare you ten seconds of their time.

So you ask yourself: *What's on people's minds? What are they most perturbed about? What are they talking about around the barbecues this Christmas?*

Hindsight tells us that this was, as they say, a no-brainer. You talk about the Treaty. But that wasn't clear to all before that speech was delivered. The party strategists would have been working on hunches to an extent, but we can safely assume that polling also helped inform their choice. This isn't to say politicians don't choose topics that sincerely exercise them and on which they will take a principled stand. But politicians with bad poll results pay special attention to issues that will help get them elected.

And so you can be confident that on 27 January 2004, by the time Don Brash cleared his throat, rose to his feet and began his delivery, a lot of preparation and strategising had gone into what was to come. Not that the media were initially sure it would make much difference. John Armstrong wrote the next day in the *New Zealand Herald*:

> Don Brash's much-hyped 'racial separatism' speech – delivered on Sir Robert's old stamping-ground of the Orewa Rotary Club – turns out to be not quite the ripsnorter required to quickly turn around National's fortunes ... Dr Brash's speech will capture minds. Whether he has captured hearts is another matter.

Well, he captured something! Helped along by a mud-splattering at Waitangi, the man was suddenly all over the media and all about the country responding to criticism ranging from indignant to withering. And for every criticism, there was an enthusiastic talkback caller saying *It's about time!*

And then on Saturday, 14 February, the first poll came out. A 16 per cent jump.

You just don't get this kind of thing, the commentators said.

This is remarkable.

Some mistake surely.

No, really, said the public in a series of following polls, *we love this stuff!*

So what was it he had said in the speech that had got everyone so excited? And why did he get so much electoral traction overnight?

Over the following weeks we saw polls, we saw TV interviews, we heard the talkback radio, and on the Internet (where I spend a good chunk of my working day) we saw a *lot* of debate – or at least a lot of assertions.

If there was a common thread, it seemed to be that Maori were getting too much that they shouldn't be getting. Just what that might be wasn't entirely clear, but the emotions and attitudes that were liberated after the Orewa speech were plain enough.

It was in the spirit of clearing a little of the confusion swirling in the immediate aftermath of 'Hurricane Brash' that a week or two after the speech, I made my own contribution. I write an online column once a week or so on things that interest me (*PublicAddress.Net*), and it struck me that the debate seemed to be suffering from an absence of facts.

I began by explaining that over the years I'd written quite a few speeches for politicians about Treaty issues. I explained that politicians approach the topic with more care than just about any. You draft and you redraft. And everyone wants to have a go at it. And I recalled two speeches I'd worked on for the Sesquicentennial in 1990. The Treaty was 150 years old; everyone was coming to Waitangi and I had spent much of that January working on speech drafts. One for the Prime Minister, one for the Queen.

I recalled that the process began in the best possible way; the then Prime Minister Geoffrey Palmer invited a few esteemed legal minds – Sir Ken Keith, John McGrath and Alex Frame among them – to talk over ideas for the speeches. We looked at themes, issues and messages, and talked about history. They were marvellous people to work with: thoughtful, insightful. You couldn't have left that meeting, I said, without feeling positive about the Treaty and the legal and academic work that was being done to consider its ramifications.

The speeches, I said, had been duly delivered in the usual atmosphere of controlled chaos associated with Waitangi Day, but the next day I'd had a real surprise. I'd got a call from a lawyer I knew who was a partner in one of the big Wellington law firms, the kind of person I would have confidently predicted would be voting for the National Party to which Winston Peters then belonged. It would be fair to say that the speeches took the liberal position that you would expect of a Labour administration, and yet he wanted me to know how much they had impressed him.

I wondered, I wrote, what he would have made of Don Brash's speech, and I speculated that if he'd had anything like the point of view I'd been encountering lately, it would have been: *excellent*. A button had been pushed, and a lot of people seemed to be responding. But what button exactly? Well, how about this: a vague notion that the Treaty process is out of control; that it's costing a fortune; that the country is being held to ransom by an endless list of Treaty demands; that Maori receive preferential treatment in countless areas of daily life.

I believe the technical legal term for these propositions is: *baseless unsubstantiated assertions*. And the trouble is, it can be hard to debate any of these issues without turning things sour. The last time it seemed this tricky was the winter of the 1981 Springbok tour. I don't know if we're any better or worse than any other nation at this, but it seems to me that we can't debate the tough issues well. We have a tendency to trade assertions and keep stating our intractable positions in increasingly loud voices. And while you're just trading unsubstantiated assertions, you're not going to get anywhere. You need some facts and some solid ideas to work with. You can't argue productively about something if you're not clear what it is you're arguing about.

To illustrate what I was talking about in my column, I put together a short online quiz for people to test their basic knowledge of Treaty issues. The aim of the exercise was actually to demonstrate that as a proportion of government money, the amount that was going on Treaty settlements was surprisingly slight. And I expanded on that by quizzing readers on a few other things, such as: how many claims had been made, what progress was being made on them, what the foreshore debate was all about, and that kind of thing.

I hadn't set out to grade the results, but within an hour or two of putting it up, people were emailing their scores and asking to know where they ranked. So I made a few changes, and included a scoring facility.

Now, it's hardly scientific, but, for what it's worth, more than 5000 people have taken the test so far. There were twelve questions, and people were largely scoring four or five correct. This was a multi-choice quiz and not especially hard, but the scores bore out what I'd suggested, that even some of the basic facts are not well known.

If we don't know precisely what it is we're arguing over, perhaps we should arm ourselves with a bundle of the relevant facts. Which just happens to be what lies ahead of us in this little guide.

This is not a grand scholarly or historical expedition – many people have done that very well already. The aim here is to set out the basic information – if you like: *Who got us into this mess, and how do we get ourselves out?*

To do that, we still have to go back and look at the history. But we'll be taking the helicopter ride, rather then covering every mile by foot, so don't expect to learn what colour hat Lieutenant Hobson was wearing at Waitangi. Instead we'll be working out why the Treaty matters, how it's been applied (or not), and what we need to do to make it work in a way that's good for us all.

Whether everyone sincerely means it when they say, *It's good we're having this debate*, the fact is, we can only get something worthwhile out of it if we know what we're talking about. This is not a problem that can't be handled. It's a tangle of issues that haven't been altogether well managed and that need to be unravelled, no doubt about that – but that *can* be done.

This is a debate, in some ways, about sharing power, and some countries end up dealing with this kind of thing in pretty bloody ways. The worst the Treaty argument has probably given anyone lately is a paper cut. In many ways, it's a bit like one of those problems that can seem huge at four o'clock in the morning, but much less worrying in the light of day.

As we'll see, a lot of anxiety about the Treaty in the last decade or so has had to do with what *might* happen rather than anything that actually has. So let's see what all the fuss is about . . .

TEST YOUR TREATY KNOWLEDGE 2

What was the approximate size of Telecom's profit for the year ending June 2003?

- **A. $481 million**
- **B. $596 million**
- **C. $709 million**
- **D. $1.23 billion**
- **E. $2.51 billion**

(Answers page 199)

CHAPTER ONE: THE NEW 'SEPARATISM'

'This is madness. Where will it end?'

> 'The cult obliges people to pretend to have faith. They must pretend to knowledge no one has. I believe more than 80 statutes require adherence to principles of the Treaty of Waitangi. There is no legislative statement of what those principles are.'
>
> ACT MP STEPHEN FRANKS

I HAVE the greatest faith in doctors, and I say that as someone who has taken himself off to them for help with everything from a broken toe to a heart attack. 'This will just hurt for a moment,' they say, and I happily roll up my sleeve.

But what if you struck one who told you that the best treatment for your headache would be brain surgery, going in from the foot?

Doctor Brash – who, of course, is a doctor of the PhD kind rather than the kind adhering to that 'First do no harm' maxim – took a diagnosis and a prescription with him to Orewa. The patient had a migraine brought on by Treaty worries, and it was time for a trip to the operating theatre. The diagnosis was not altogether wrong, but was he serious about the treatment? Let's look at what he had to say, and then see how it lines up with what had been happening.

He said he saw a 'dangerous drift towards racial separatism in New Zealand, and the development of the now entrenched Treaty grievance industry'. He saw us becoming a racially divided nation, with two sets of laws, and two standards of citizenship. Why? Well, because, he said, we were putting racial distinctions into large parts of our legislation. We were funding people's education and healthcare on the basis not just of need, but also by the ethnicity of the recipient.

None of us was around at the time of the New Zealand Wars, he said. None of us had anything to do with the confiscations: 'There is a limit to how much any generation can apologise for the sins of its great-grandparents.' He thought too many Maori leaders were looking backwards rather than towards the future, and that too many have been encouraged by successive governments to adopt grievance mode.

And he wasn't best pleased about the 'principles of the Treaty'.

> These principles were never defined – nobody had a clue what they might be. In the end, it was left to unelected Court of Appeal judges to determine an interpretation of the Treaty's meaning that the politicians most certainly never intended ... governments have included references to the 'principles of the Treaty' in legislation, still without defining them.

He doubted the Treaty had anything to say about ...

> ... today's SOEs and national parks, today's schools and universities, how we go about approving or declining building permits, what science we should study, what art we should look

> at, and even how we should regard the new frontier of genetic science!

He was worried about local authorities introducing Maori wards 'without regard to whether the guiding democratic principle of "one person, one vote, one value" is violated'. And he thought Maori had an unfair influence: 'They possess the power to veto many development projects, projects which could provide us all with jobs.

'We fly Maori elders around the world to lift tapu and expel evil spirits from New Zealand embassies; we allow courts to become entangled in hearings about the risks to taniwha of a new road or building,' he said, and he was especially upset about consultation payments:

> This process is becoming deeply corrupt, with some requirements for consultation resulting in substantial payments in a system that looks like nothing other than standover tactics.

In summary, he thought the Treaty of Waitangi should not be used as the basis for giving greater civil, political or democratic rights to any particular ethnic group.

> We intend to remove divisive race-based features from legislation. The 'principles of the Treaty' – never clearly defined yet ever expanding – are the thin end of a wedge leading to a racially divided state and we want no part of that. There can be no basis for special privileges for any race, no basis for government funding based on race, no basis for introducing Maori wards in local authority elections, and no obligation for local governments to consult Maori in preference to other New Zealanders.

Oh, and while we're at it: 'We will remove the anachronism of the Maori seats in Parliament.' (Actually he had a bit to say about the foreshore, too, but we'll come to that later.)

There seem to be five main issues raised by Brash that we need to consider:

- **Interpreting the Treaty** – What does this 'nineteenth-century document', as Brash describes it – mean today?
- **Consultation** – What should we make of the obligations that legislation puts on people to consult Maori about various things?
- **Preferential rights** – Do Maori get benefits that other New Zealanders don't? Should they?
- **Biculturalism** – What about all those 'bizarre' things we keep doing like sending Maori to lift tapu on buildings? Have we got that right?
- **Power sharing** – How does this business of voting rights and representation on boards and councils work?

While trying to make some sense of all this, it's also worth bearing in mind that aspects of this business have unfolded within government and the bureaucracy in haphazard and sometimes unlikely ways. By the end of the 1980s, two important factors were influencing the way such issues were being handled. The state was steadily developing policies of biculturalism – meaning that your typical government department was doing what it could to acknowledge that there was a Maori culture as well as a Pakeha one to be recognised.

By now, because of the *Lands* case, the Court of Appeal had advised that Pakeha had a partner, forcing the issue: *If we're in partnership – how do we go about that?* It would have some interesting consequences.

Work your way around the politicians today and you'll find one aspect that most of them agree on: that one word, 'partnership', created a whole world of trouble.

Was it the wrong word to use? Michael Cullen thinks it was, and that it had all kinds of unexpected effects.

> The partnership word *has* been a very dangerous word because it's led to expectations. And the partnership thing has sort of said, 'Right, this is the Crown and Maori and we govern the country in this partnership so it's an equal voice with effective veto power.' Pakeha are saying, 'Like bloody hell, it's one person, one vote, etc., etc.'
>
> It's grown like topsy – absolutely layer upon layer. You've got the bureaucrats going off the deep end because they want to cover themselves. I suspect some – because they think the Government's sort of so PC – go overboard in their own responses, otherwise we'll be upset. They're hopelessly eager to please, getting carried away. And some smart operators within Maoridom recognise they can really take people for a ride on this, and you know there are some good operators within there – conmen might be too strong a word, but there are some absolute crackers – and now we're saying, 'What the hell is going on here?'

John Tamihere believes some bureaucrats have been taken for a bit of a ride by 'a lot of born-again Horis down here who've made a very good killing out of the so-called consultancy racket'. He says that anyone remaking an organisation to recognise Treaty principles has major problems because they're starting from nothing.

> There's no manual. And who do you get to write the manual? The very person who's going to continue to make money out of having to write the manual . . . So I just say a number of the new breed of Horis have rorted that and made it difficult for us. And that's not a Pakeha problem, okay? You give them an opening for a rort and you get a rort. And a lot of that's happened lately, and it needs to be hunted down and sorted.

Margaret Wilson puts it a little more gently:

> … People had to find practical expression of what partnership meant and because notions of equality are quite strong in New Zealand it was seen as 50/50. Now this of course led to some ridiculous situations, because you haven't got enough people to go around and you haven't got enough competencies to go around and it's not also necessary to actually divide it up like that in terms of the activity.
>
> So I think it's true that bureaucracies were finding and struggling for more practical ways to give expression to a notion that was really ill-defined. And I think that probably has led to things that just can't work in practice. And therefore they fall into disrepute.

Harsher critics might say that we've ended up with a lot of behaviour in government departments and schools and educational institutions that seems to be a sort of shorthand way of saying, 'Let's be nice to Maori'. They see the forces of 'political correctness' intimidating the majority from speaking out. In those terms, Brash's speech seemed to them to be official permission that it was okay to say you didn't agree with all this.

Of course, to even enter the debate about where the Treaty process and race relations have arrived at in modern New Zealand, it is unavoidable that we must retrace some of the steps our forebears – Maori and Pakeha – took as they did what we're doing now: making it up as we go along.

CHAPTER TWO: ARRIVAL TIMES

'I'll tell you what they had when we got here. Nothing. They were running around in grass skirts, killing and eating each other.'

HOW BRAVE do you have to be to sail out over a lagoon somewhere in East Polynesia and into a vast ocean, knowing you may never come back? How able a mariner do you have to be to ride thousands of kilometres across the Pacific, guided only by stars, ocean swells and currents? Some time in the thirteenth century – and we can thank carbon dating for telling us this – navigators like those became the first New Zealanders.

If you learned about them from the same school lessons I did, you'll recall that they arrived here a few centuries earlier than 1300 AD, and discovered the Morioris living here. Well, actually, no. Historian Michael King did a lot to help clarify this. Carbon dating and DNA from kiore – not to mention physical features and the tools and language they had in common – have helped explain things. Of that group of East Polynesians who reached New Zealand in the thirteenth century, a group made another voyage some time in the fourteenth or fifteenth century which took them on to the Chatham Islands. They settled there, and by the time Maori from the mainland encountered them again in the nineteenth century, all memory of them had gone. If your teacher told you that Maori sailed to Aotearoa and colonised the Moriori, you can ask to have your paper regraded. It didn't happen.

For the first hundred or so years, the new settlers did what many new settlers have done – they piled into the supplies. Moa, large birds, seals all made good – and, by all accounts, pretty easy – meat. These were creatures that didn't have much experience of being hunted. Of course, if you don't have a sustainable hunting approach, sooner or later, there'll be nothing left. A few species disappeared. The settlers moved on to Plan B. For some, this meant hunter-gathering, for others it meant settling in one place and growing food. That usually meant working in larger groups to cultivate the crops, and led to the communal tribal life that was in place by the time Europeans arrived here.

Over time they adapted to their new environment. They developed their own specific culture, practices, customs and beliefs. Living as a group was a very important part of that: the interest of the tribe came first. They cultivated, they fished, they caught birds, they traded, they shared a common language, they shared common values, and from time to time they fought – fiercely and with skill. That's not to say that they were perpetually at war with one another. You would fight to redress an imbalance, you might fight for territory, but you might also be a long while without it.

By the time the first Europeans arrived here, those sailors from East Polynesia had been here for perhaps 500 years. Which brings us to the point where a very smart race of people arrives and everything changes. Or not. We should pause for a moment for the *Guns, Germs and Steel* view of history, because it's a pretty helpful one. Jared Diamond is a historian who was intrigued by the questions: Why did history unfold differently on different continents? Why did people of Eurasian origin come to dominate the modern world in wealth and power? Why did human development proceed at different rates in different places? He found that if you explore that question you'll see that people have tended to confuse a race's *state* of development with their *capacity* for development.

In essence, it depends on which spot of the globe you happened to be in. Eurasia had the best combination of factors. It had the best environment for food production. That high capacity for food production created spare capacity to do other things – developing writing and technology. That created the opportunity to send out fleets of conquest and exploration. So you get one race doing better than another, not because they're biologically superior, but because they started out in the right spot. The right environment gave them the spare capacity to build and grow and develop. Of course, if you'd tried that out on the British in the Colonial Office they'd have laughed you out of the room. They knew all about the White Man's Burden. Europeans who arrived here thinking they were dealing with 'savages' who would not easily adapt to 'civilised' ways were in for a surprise. As we'll see, it took a long time for some of them to let go of the idea. If you take the pessimistic view, you might say that some still haven't.

They wouldn't have been wrong to declare that their impact on Maori would be colossal, though. By the time Captain Cook was charting New Zealand, there were possibly 100,000 Maori here. Over the next seventy years, the number of Europeans actually living here would build only slowly, up to about 2000 in 1840. But the exchange between the cultures began quickly, and had a very significant impact.

By 1800, the ships were becoming regular. European seamen would sail into the harbours to rest up and take on supplies, and Maori were soon trading with them. There was something in it for both sides. Maori provided supplies and services in exchange for implements and weapons, muskets, tools, clothing, blankets. Until then, they'd grown crops just for their own needs. Now they began cultivating crops to supply the traders. A range of new activities sprung up – timber, flax, shore-whaling, ship-building and general trading. Maori would meet an interesting selection of types from this new world. Sealers and whalers first, then missionaries, then traders. They adapted in many ways as they came to know the ways of life of these new people. The missionaries brought their Bibles, their churches and literacy, and new ideas about ways of living: the way they traded, the way they organised their society, the way they administered justice. It wasn't long before Maori were working the ships and taking opportunities to see the world. They travelled to Australia, to Britain, and they brought back new ideas and new ways of thinking about the world.

And then, of course, there were the muskets. Tribes weren't slow to see the advantage these weapons would give them. They armed themselves and set about settling old scores and claiming land. Possibly as many as 30,000 had died by the time the weapons were held widely and a kind of balance of terror restored some order.

Right up until the signing of the Treaty, Maori were unquestionably in control of the country, and for some years after, they were still the greater economic force. By the mid-1830s they were trading wheat and butter extensively. Their agriculture thrived. Not only were they supplying most of the food for Pakeha but they were also exporting surplus food to Australia. In fact, the export business to Australia was substantial enough for them to start up a ship-building industry. As they gained literacy, the opportunities for trading with Europeans continued to expand.

As all this was going on, Britain, of course, was going about the important business of creating an empire on which the sun would never set. But they were paying substantially more attention to bigger parts of the globe like Australia and Canada and Africa than they were to New Zealand. It was only as trouble started to brew over the things British subjects were doing here – all the way from general lawlessness to murders of a Maori chief and his family – that they gave much thought to having some kind of presence here. Their first real move was to appoint James Busby to act as British Resident in New Zealand.

He arrived in May 1833 and set up a Residency at Waitangi. Although he was really a policeman with a helmet and whistle but no jail or truncheon, he gave it his best shot, and he made some quite impressive efforts to try to help Maori set up some kind of governing structure. In 1835 he helped a confederation of chiefs to produce a Declaration of Independence which was initially signed by thirty-four, and by fifty-two in the end. It declared that all sovereign power and authority in the land resided with the chiefs 'in their collective capacity', expressed as the United Tribes of New Zealand. They declared they would meet annually to make laws.

How much weight you put on this document depends on who's telling the story. Maori sovereignty advocates rate it highly, but you won't get that point of view from everyone. What it means for the purpose of this story is that Busby could see it wasn't going to do the trick as far as effective government goes. Meanwhile other parties were starting to think that some form of government was going to be necessary.

Since the beginning of the 1830s, chiefs had been asking Britain – from time to time – to bring the British subjects under the control of the Crown. By the end of the 1830s you had about 2000 permanent Pakeha residents here, and the more law-abiding of them were starting to fret. They wanted some kind of government to keep things in order and there wasn't one of any kind that they could see. There was plenty to be fretting about, and back home in Britain the Colonial Office was coming to the same point of view.

As well as lawlessness, there was also a fast-growing problem with land sales. Talk had started to build that Britain might soon make some sort of move on New Zealand. A few people looked at that and saw the chance to make a killing: buy up land now and then sell it once the Government moves in, takes over the land and issues a good title. They started buying, although what they thought they were buying and what Maori perceived themselves to have been selling may well have been different things. The issue got the British Government worried, so much so that the House of Lords held an inquiry in 1838. The upshot was that they looked down the road, saw confrontation and violence not too far ahead, and felt that Something Should Be Done. Add to that the plans of The New Zealand Association, for one, which intended to set up a New Zealand colony, and you have a lot of pressure building.

Now this is where it gets especially interesting. As we read the story ahead we'll see that what followed would be best described as colonisation. But there are ways and ways of colonising, and thanks in part to the influence of 'humanitarian' thinkers in Britain, this one was going to end up being handled a little differently from some earlier examples. In fact, the humanitarian point of view was that you shouldn't be colonising and settling. Everywhere Britain had gone, it had proved to be injurious to the good health of an indigenous people. Humanitarians thought colonisation and settlement of New Zealand would be dangerous, and best avoided. The Government tended to agree: better to trade with the country than colonise and settle it.

But their opinion shifted as the pressure built, and by 1839 they were ready to act. Lieutenant-Governor William Hobson was sent to New Zealand with instructions from the Colonial Secretary, Lord Normanby, to acquire sovereignty over New Zealand. His instructions were very strong on one point in particular:

> All dealings with the Aborigines for their lands must be conducted on the same principles of sincerity, justice and good faith as must govern your transactions with them for the recognition of Her Majesty's Sovereignty in the Islands. Nor is this all. They must not be permitted to enter into any Contracts in which they might be the ignorant and unintentional authors of injuries to themselves. You will not, for example, purchase from them any territory the retention of which by them would be essential, or highly conducive, to their own comfort, safety or subsistence. The acquisition of Land by the Crown for the future settlements of British subjects must be combined to such districts as the natives can alienate without distress or serious inconvenience to themselves. To secure the observance of this rule will be one of the first duties of their official protector …

By the end of January 1840, Hobson's ship was dropping anchor in the Bay of Islands and the Colonial Office was about to try a new approach to colonisation.

TEST YOUR TREATY KNOWLEDGE 3

How much revenue did the New Zealand Government collect for the year ending June 2003?

A. $8 billion
B. $23 billion
C. $36 billion
D. $46 billion
E. $57 billion

(Answers page 199)

'There were about half a dozen different versions of that thing. No one knew what they were signing.'

LESS IS more, it has been said. And there is certainly beauty in simplicity. Being longer doesn't necessarily imply that a document has greater meaning or significance, as the following list might suggest:

- The Lord's Prayer: 66 words
- The Ten Commandments: 179 words
- The US Declaration of Independence: 1300 words
- EU regulations on duck eggs: 26,911 words

Well, no complaints about the Treaty of Waitangi on that score. It won't take you long to read it. We have two versions here for you. Yes, there were a number of other copies made that weren't quite the same, but let's just deal with the core issues here. We'll start by looking at the English and Maori versions that were presented on the lawn at Waitangi, 5 February 1840.

Preamble

HER MAJESTY VICTORIA Queen of the United Kingdom of Great Britain and Ireland regarding with Her Royal Favour the Native Chiefs and Tribes of New Zealand and anxious to protect their just Rights and Property and to secure to them the enjoyment of Peace and Good Order has deemed it necessary in consequence of the great number of Her Majesty's Subjects who have already settled in New Zealand and the rapid extension of Emigration both from Europe and Australia which is still in progress to constitute and appoint a functionary properly authorised to treat with the Aborigines of New Zealand for the recognition of Her Majesty's Sovereign authority over the whole or any part of those islands – Her Majesty therefore being desirous to establish a settled form of Civil Government with a view to avert the evil consequences which must result from the absence of the necessary Laws and Institutions alike to the native population and to Her subjects has been graciously pleased to empower and to authorise me William Hobson a Captain in Her Majesty's Royal Navy Consul and Lieutenant-Governor of such parts of New Zealand as may be or hereafter shall be ceded to her Majesty to invite the confederated and independent Chiefs of New Zealand to concur in the following Articles and Conditions.	KO WIKITORIA te Kuini o Ingarani i tana mahara atawai ki nga Rangatira me nga Hapu o Nu Tirani i tana hiahia hoki kia tohungia ki a ratou o ratou rangatiratanga me to ratou wenua, a kia mau tonu hoki te Rongo ki a ratou me te Atanoho hoki kua wakaaro ia he mea tika kia tukua mai tetahi Rangatira – hei kai wakarite ki nga Tangata maori o Nu Tirani – kia wakaaetia e nga Rangatira Maori te Kawanatanga o te Kuini ki nga wahikatoa o te wenua nei me nga motu – na te mea hoki he tokomaha ke nga tangata o tona Iwi Kua noho ki tenei wenua, a e haere mai nei. Na ko te Kuini e hiahia ana kia wakaritea te Kawanatanga kia kaua ai nga kino e puta mai ki te tangata Maori ki te Pakeha e noho ture kore ana. Na kua pai te Kuini kia tukua a hau a Wiremu Hopihona he Kapitana i te Roiara Nawi hei Kawana mo nga wahi katoa o Nu Tirani e tukua aianei amua atu ki te Kuini, e mea atu ana ia ki nga Rangatira o te wakaminenga o nga hapu o Nu Tirani me era Rangatira atu enei ture ka korerotia nei.

Article the First	Ko te Tuatahi
The Chiefs of the Confederation of the United Tribes of New Zealand and the separate and independent Chiefs who have not become members of the Confederation cede to Her Majesty the Queen of England absolutely and without reservation all the rights and powers of Sovereignty which the said Confederation or Individual Chiefs respectively exercise or possess, or may be supposed to exercise or to possess over their respective Territories as the sole sovereigns thereof.	Ko nga Rangatira o te wakaminenga me nga Rangatira katoa hoki ki hai i uru ki taua wakaminenga ka tuku rawa atu ki te Kuini o Ingarani ake tonu atu – te Kawanatanga katoa o o ratou wenua.
Article the Second	**Ko te Tuarua**
Her Majesty the Queen of England confirms and guarantees to the Chiefs and Tribes of New Zealand and to the respective families and individuals thereof the full exclusive and undisturbed possession of their Lands and Estates Forests Fisheries and other properties which they may collectively or individually possess so long as it is their wish and desire to retain the same in their possession; but the Chiefs of the United Tribes and the individual Chiefs yield to Her Majesty the exclusive right of Preemption over such lands as the proprietors thereof may be disposed to alienate at such prices as may be agreed upon between the respective Proprietors and persons appointed by Her Majesty to treat with them in that behalf.	Ko te Kuini o Ingarani ka wakarite ka wakaae ki nga Rangitira ki nga hapu – ki nga tangata katoa o Nu Tirani te tino rangatiratanga o o ratou wenua o ratou kainga me o ratou taonga katoa. Otiia ko nga Rangatira o te wakaminenga me nga Rangatira katoa atu ka tuku ki te Kuini te hokonga o era wahi wenua e pai ai te tangata nona te Wenua – ki te ritenga o te utu e wakaritea ai e ratou ko te kai hoko e meatia nei e te Kuini hei kai hoko mona.
Article the Third	**Ko te Tuatoru**
In consideration thereof Her Majesty the Queen of England extends to the Natives of New Zealand Her royal protection and imparts to them all the Rights and Privileges of British Subjects. *(signed)* **William Hobson,** Consul and Lieutenant-Governor.	Hei wakaritenga mai hoki tenei mo te wakaaetanga ki te Kawanatanga o te Kuini – Ka tiakina e te Kuini o Ingarani nga tangata maori katoa o Nu Tirani ka tukua ki a ratou nga tikanga katoa rite tahi ki ana mea ki nga tangata o Ingarani. *(signed)* **William Hobson,** Consul and Lieutenant-Governor.

Now therefore We the Chiefs of the Confederation of the United Tribes of New Zealand being assembled in Congress at Victoria in Waitangi and We the Separate and Independent Chiefs of New Zealand claiming authority over the Tribes and Territories which are specified after our respective names, having been made fully to understand the Provisions of the foregoing Treaty, accept and enter into the same in the full spirit and meaning thereof in witness of which we have attached our signatures or marks at the places and the dates respectively specified. Done at Waitangi this Sixth day of February in the year of Our Lord one thousand eight hundred and forty.	Na ko matou ko nga Rangatira o te Wakaminenga o nga hapu o Nu Tirani ka huihui nei ki Waitangi ko matou hoki ko nga Rangatira o Nu Tirani ka kite nei i te ritenga o enei kupu, ka tangohia ka wakaaetia katoatia e matou, koia ka tohungia ai o matou ingoa o matou tohu. Ka meatia tenei ki Waitangi i te ono o nga ra o Pepueri i te tau kotahi mano, e waru rau e wa te kau o to tatou Ariki.

I'm all for brevity. But you have to be careful how you use it. A cut too many can leave your meaning a little. If you get my drift. On the one hand, it will keep you focused on the essence of the idea; on the other it may not cover everything you want to convey.

If you've read the story of the creation of the United States Constitution, you'll know that days can turn into weeks, weeks into months, and months into years when you try to work out something as fundamental as the framework for governing your country. The drafting of the Treaty of Waitangi was an altogether different proposition. But then, if you'd asked the Colonial Office, it's unlikely they'd have said they saw it in those terms. Hobson wrote out some notes over a few days. He showed them to Busby (who was also organising a meeting of chiefs on 5 February) who thought it needed more, and added a good deal, including the promise in Article II that Britain would guarantee Maori possession of their *Lands and Estates Forests Fisheries and other properties*. He knew them: there would be no deal without that. The Treaty had to be translated, of course. The missionary Henry Williams and his son Edward did so on the evening of 4 February. The result was a treaty which purported, essentially, to do this:

> It recognised that Maori were the prior occupants.
>
> It made it possible for the Crown to set up a government.
>
> It guaranteed to Maori that their tribal authority over their lands, fisheries, forests, villages, treasures and culture would be protected.
>
> It made it possible for the Crown (and only the Crown) to buy land from Maori, if they wished to sell it, and sell it to settlers.
>
> It gave everyone, settlers and Maori, the status and rights of British citizens.

However – and you knew that word had to be coming – the difference in translation caused some ambiguity.

In Article I we read in English that Maori ceded sovereignty to the Queen. But do we find that in the Maori version? The closest equivalent to sovereignty might be 'mana' or 'rangatiratanga' but instead it uses 'kawanatanga', which means governorship. That suggests not so much that Maori have passed authority over to the British, but rather that they've enabled the setting up of a government by the British.

Then in Article II: the Maori text, in exchange for the protection of the Queen, gave Maori people 'unqualified exercise of their chieftainship (te tino rangatiratanga) over their lands, villages and all their treasures (taonga)'. That looks a good deal more like shared authority. It suggests that they would keep their control over tribal matters.

The Maori text with the use of 'te tino rangatiratanga' has a much wider meaning than the English text, which guarantees to the Maori: 'the full, exclusive and undisturbed possession of their lands and estates, forests, fisheries, and other properties'. And there's one crucial word there: 'taonga'. Property and possessions won't do it: it's *all* things held precious, and that would turn out to be pretty significant a century and a half later.

Time for some expert help here. The first lecturer I had at law school who taught our class anything Treaty-related was Alex Frame. He grew up in Tahiti, learning to speak Tahitian fluently – an advantage, he says, when it came to understanding Maori later in his career. He trained in law, becoming a lecturer, and early in his academic career in the 1970s began introducing material into the courses that he was teaching. 'I can remember when one used to get sort of whistled for it from the back rows of very large law classes.' That continued through the 1970s, and when he came back to New Zealand, he found himself building more and more of the Treaty work. Then he began advising Maori groups on various matters and was involved in the first of the modern Tribunal hearings – Motunui – in 1983. In 1988 he was asked to head up the Treaty of Waitangi unit in the Ministry of Justice; so from being a commentator and a teacher on the Treaty he moved to responsibilities of advising government.

> People sometimes ask me, 'How do I see the Treaty. How should we think of the Treaty?'
>
> I've always said that the first article of the Treaty – the kawanatanga part – is very strong – much stronger than some Maori are prepared to concede, and the second article, which guarantees rangatiratanga is also very strong – much stronger than many Pakeha are prepared to concede.
>
> So how can we have these two strong articles sitting there? I'm tempted sometimes by this idea. In a way both sides gambled. The Crown gambled. Why was it prepared to sign up to Article II? Well, in a sense the Crown gambled that

> there would be assimilation. And therefore if there was assimilation, as you will see, Article II would become increasingly unimportant. On the other hand, Maori gambled. After all, why did Maori sign up for Article I – and by the way, don't go for these readings that say Article I was only giving the Queen power over Pakeha. The most elementary reading of the Maori version of the first article shows that that is completely untenable. It gives the Queen te Kawanatanga katoa – all – of the kawanatanga; o ratou wenua – of their lands. Now, which lands is that? That's the lands of the chiefs. That's all it can be – have a look at the structure and I challenge anyone to show me an even faintly tenable reading which can dispute that it's all the territory of New Zealand.
>
> So why did Maori sign up to that? Well, I think they gambled. I think they gambled that the demographics in New Zealand would stay, not exactly as they were in 1840, but would stay approximately such that there would be a preponderance of Maori and that the newcomers would be relatively few. I know there is a reference in the preamble to others coming, but I think the gamble was that if the demographics stayed favourable to Maori then this kawanatanga thing would be a really abstract sort of notion in the background.

We'll be coming back to this later, but it's also worth bearing in mind that as much as you need to find out what the words mean, and what the parties understood them to mean, it's also important to keep the broad perspective that asks: who was signing this, why were they signing this, and what did they expect? As Alex Frame says, there was a bit of a gamble going on here on both sides.

Sir Douglas Graham takes the view that you must keep the big picture in mind.

> I remember going down to Waikato University to give a lecture … somebody asked me a question at the end: 'Which version of the Treaty should we follow?' I said, 'Who cares? If you've got time and you're an academic and you've got nothing else to do,

> well you could compare this word here with that word over there, but it's all silly, you know, it's all a waste of time really.' What does the Treaty actually *mean* in the big picture? Don't worry about the Maori version of fisheries or taonga or something – what's it mean *today?* We're in 2004, for goodness' sake, not 1844. So unless it's practical, you know, I really don't have much time for it. Oh, they were flabbergasted. Aghast. They'd spent months on this. So perhaps I shouldn't have said that.

He makes a good point, though. Sometimes we can't see the wood for the, well, forests and fisheries.

Let's look at how the Treaty was presented to the chiefs. The proposition was that the Queen was concerned for both Maori and Pakeha because of the lack of law and order. Would rangatira agree to Hobson becoming the Governor? He would then be able to control the British settlers. Busby told them that Hobson was not going to take away their land but, rather, keep it safe from settlers. They stressed Article II: 'your position and authority is recognised and protected'.

It was debated for hours. Would they retain their lands? Would their tribal authority and status be protected? They knew that the settlers were going to get land, and they knew they needed protection. Opinions were divided. You had chiefs like Te Ruki Kawiti of Nga Puhi saying: 'No. No. Go back, what do you want here? We native men do not wish you to stay. We do not want to be tied up and trodden down. We are free!' On the other hand you had Tamati Waka Nene, also of Nga Puhi, saying it was too late. 'Many of his children are also our tamariki. He makes no slaves.' He talked about trade and preserving the friendship that had been built.

Remember, it was the Maori text that was discussed. Sovereignty was not ceded in this text, and the chiefs who signed on 6 February 1840, and in all other places except the

Waikato, signed the Maori text. Their main concerns seem to have been about their authority (power and control), their land, and trade dealings. Their impression seemed to be that there would be a sharing of authority in the land, which would enhance their mana. The Governor would protect the country and control Pakeha.

Historian Dame Anne Salmond says that in her view the treaty that counts is the one that was negotiated and signed, which was the treaty in Maori.

> That makes a huge difference, that in that period, the common language was Maori, not English. The English translation of the Treaty, if you like, was an interesting artefact, but it's not the one that was signed.
>
> The thing about the text is that if you read it in the language in which it was expressed, and finally written, what seems to be going on was a kind of chiefly gift exchange. There is this language – the use of tuku, which is the language of giving, handing over to somebody something precious. The rangatira are giving things over to the Queen and [the] Queen is offering to them certain guarantees. It has got this very ceremonial, respectful language. This was a relationship which was being forged and gifts were being exchanged. In that way of thinking, those relationships were based on mana. You were supposed to honour them [and] people expected Queen Victoria to continue to honour those agreements because they were personal to that genealogical line, if you like.
>
> So when you look at it that way, you can see why people signed it. Because it appeared that on the one hand they were letting the Queen have a Governor and that would mediate the relationship, and they would forge a relationship with someone they would have said was a high rangatira. Their own chiefly rights were explicitly protected. Then they were going to have [exactly] the same tikanga as the people in England. Look at it that way, and understand it in that language, that was a pretty good deal.

Remember, too, the bargaining position – this was an agreement between a small band of foreigners and the chiefs of the tribes of 60,000 strong, brave, smart people. Yes, they saw other people coming, but they were still in a position of strength. More settlement would mean more markets, more trade. That had been going very well for them: why would they not want to see more, as long as their position of strength was retained?

This was an agreement between two peoples, both seeing some purpose in sharing the same space and both needing to find acceptable terms for sharing it.

In due course, Hobson gathered signatures from chiefs throughout the North Island. On 21 May 1840, to head off the New Zealand Company beating him to it, he proclaimed British sovereignty over the North Island 'by cession' and over the South Island 'by discovery' – meaning before anyone in the South Island was even asked, although in due course the Treaty was taken there and signed. A new regime was under way.

Sir Douglas Graham has written that the greatest fault of the Treaty was that it didn't write into it an institution to deal with breaches. Anne Salmond agrees that some mechanism for handling breaches might have helped:

> ... When the Treaty was signed and negotiated, you had tribal chiefs, rangatira, who used to go round making peace with each other. Probably we needed some agent or agency like that. I think that people really did expect the Crown to honour those promises, as you would, because of the serious way in which the Treaty was negotiated in the first place.
>
> A lot of people lost their land in Scotland and relocated to places like New Zealand, and the irony is that many of the Scots then helped perform exactly the same operation on Maori. But certainly there were always people who reminded people of the dishonour of what was going on. Sir William Martin, for example, and even some of the generals who were sent out from

> Britain, writing despatches back and saying, 'This is a travesty of justice,' so there has always been a conscience, but the problem is that those particular people were just individuals expressing, and there was no power given to that. That sense of the need to be just. To be honourable.

In any transaction you can think you know what you've signed up for, but if it goes wrong, what opportunity do you have to protest and get a ruling on whether the deal's been broken? A deal that has no remedy mechanism is a pretty poor one, and as Maori were about to discover, it would have terrible consequences for them.

TEST YOUR TREATY KNOWLEDGE 4

Of all the money the New Zealand Government has spent in the last five years, what proportion of that has been spent on Treaty settlements?

A. 0.109 per cent
B. 1.3 per cent
C. 3.23 per cent
D. 8.7 per cent
E. 16.1 per cent

(Answers page 199)

CHAPTER FOUR: BAD FAITH

'There was a war. We won it. End of story.'

> Now in making purchases from the natives I ever represented to them that though the money payment might be small, their chief recompense would lie in the kindness of the Govt. towards them, the erection & maintenance of schools & hospitals for their benefit & so on – you know it all.
>
> COMMISSIONER OF CROWN LANDS, OTAGO, MADE TO THE COLONIAL SECRETARY ON 18 MARCH 1856

THERE'S A bowling club in our neighbourhood that sits on a leafy street with pretty impressive harbour views. Just the kind of location that makes a real estate agent's heart skip a beat. A decade or more ago when we moved in, there were many old people in our street. A few of them would get into their whites once a week and make their way down to the club to have a game and chat with friends. But as the years went by, their numbers got fewer, and one day there was a story in the local paper about the troubles the club was having. There were about seventeen active members left, and there was a split vote over their future – whether or not to amalgamate with another club or something of that sort.

It occurred to me that their biggest problem might not actually be within the club, but outside. Suppose a property developer should spot an opportunity to muscle in? Some bowling clubs are on leasehold land, but this one, apparently, was freehold. What say the developer were to round up three or four dozen compliant associates and join the club – enough to form the necessary majority – and then vote to close down the club and make some money on the property? A bit far-fetched, sure, but it wouldn't necessarily be the most outrageous thing we've heard of a property developer doing in New Zealand. The land would be so valuable that they could get a tidy profit and divide up the proceeds amongst the members. Fortunately, it didn't happen. The members decided to add a pétanque facility, they had a bit of a membership drive, and today, things are running along nicely.

But if you think for a minute in those terms, about how the members of the bowling club might have felt if the developer had taken over, you might have an idea of how it felt for Maori to watch things unfolding in the first few decades after they signed the Treaty of Waitangi.

As we just saw, Maori had taken something of a gamble in signing away sovereignty, by whatever term you define it. It put a degree of power out of their hands. If there were to be a great many settlers arriving, they might not, in theory, have enough power to defend their interests, no matter what the Treaty guaranteed.

They signed the document, trusting that the numbers wouldn't hurt them, but they were wrong. As colonisation unfolded, they would discover that sovereignty meant that the new arrivals could set up a government, pass laws, act on them, and even if some of those laws contravened the rights under the Treaty, you wouldn't necessarily have any comeback on that. Why? Because the law said then – and still largely does – that the terms of a treaty don't have effect until Parliament takes those terms (even though the Crown has signed it), writes it into legislation and passes it as the law of the land. Maori had a treaty that declared their rights, but getting those rights enshrined in law was another matter. In time they would find that it wasn't actually possible to get the justice they were after.

Things didn't all go wrong in an instant. In fact, the first decade or so was in many ways a good one for Maori. At the outset, the Treaty figured very largely in everyone's thinking: Maori, the Governor, Britain, the missionaries, settlers. That's not to say that all those parties approved of it – settlers who wanted to get their hands on land bristled at it, for example, and while the Governors recognised how vital it was that the rights of the Treaty were recognised and honoured, in Britain, as policy was being formed, there were points at which certain key people would be asking with some surprise, 'It doesn't mean *that*, surely?' Well, yes, it did. This was a treaty that had taken a much more accommodating point of view than anything they had done previously. And well it might; for the better part of that first decade, Maori had the weight of numbers, and continued to represent a much stronger force than the Governor, his small band of men, whatever troops might be shipped in, and the settlers could hope to muster.

The power structure as the colony took its first steps was quite simple. The Government was, in effect, one man – the Governor – who worked with the help of a legislative council, and who took his instructions from London. He had a Land Claims Commissioner, who had the task of reviewing land deals made before the Treaty and setting them aside or recasting them where he deemed that appropriate. He appointed a Protector of Aborigines whose task was, in effect, to ensure that Treaty obligations were being honoured and that the interests of Maori were being protected. The Protector also had the job of helping the Government buy land. If you think that you probably wouldn't want to make your real estate agent a trustee of your family trust as well, you'll get an idea of the potential difficulties this created.

The process of building a system of government duly got under way. The Governor set about making and enforcing laws which Maori, to some degree, were happy to work with, but not to the extent that it cut across chiefly power. The Colonial Office looked at the problem and came to the view that Maori were subject to British sovereignty, but that in certain circumstances Maori custom should be allowed to prevail. It didn't take long for tensions to build on that point. Settlers argued that if Maori wanted to enjoy the rights of British subjects under Article III, they couldn't 'cherry-pick' and ignore the aspects that didn't suit them. They saw, however, that the Government wasn't strong enough to lay down the law, and Maori, for their part, saw that the alternative source of power was undermining chiefly authority and gradually they lost faith in government and fell back on their own ways of handling problems.

You can see the seeds here for two significant developments further down the track. On the one hand, the settlers would end up making policy on the basis that it would be best for Maori if they were absorbed into the new settler society. On the other, Maori would grow more discontented and support the notion of some kind of self-government for themselves. That, in some respects, is an argument we're still having.

For all that, though, the relationship Maori had with the Governor was effective in keeping the Treaty high in everyone's mind. You complain to the Governor, you get action. Maori could, and would, point to an action with reference to the Treaty. The Colonial Office continued to insist that the terms of the Treaty should be observed in letters to Governors Hobson, FitzRoy and Grey.

The principal question, inevitably, was land. The Government controlled the process by exercising the right of preemption that was set out in the Treaty. That made them the only game in town; Maori could only sell to them. They were able to buy cheap and sell dear, like any good speculator, with the profits going to pay the cost of setting up the new system of government. In other words, Maori ended up paying the bill for a government that, in due course, would substantially fail to protect their rights under the Treaty.

There were other reasons for having the system, as well. The idea was that by controlling the process, the Government could ensure that Maori would not be cheated. But all the while, settlers were arriving and wanting to buy land. They could see that with the Government out of the way, they would have more chance of getting land, and more than likely at a better price. In 1844, Governor FitzRoy bowed to the pressure and dropped the exclusive right, on a number of conditions: you paid a duty of 10 shillings per acre; the sale had to be approved by Protectors; and there were certain sacred sites that couldn't be sold. Sales were slow at that rate: 600 acres. He dropped the duty to a penny per acre and business boomed: 100,000 acres.

Did the Colonial Office like it? They did not. Revenue was down, and so were the profits. They told the new Governor Grey to reinstate the exclusive right, which he did, under the Native Land Purchase Ordinance of 1846. He then went on over the next eight years to buy no fewer than 32 million acres of land for fifty thousand pounds – largely in the South Island. This was good news for the government accounts, but not such good news for Maori. They had fairly quickly come to see that land sales were not necessarily going to do them great good, and they became more reluctant to sell.

In the twenty years from 1844, Ngai Tahu signed formal land sale contracts with the Crown for some 34.5 million acres, approximately 80 per cent of the South Island. In return, the Crown was to allocate one-tenth of the land to the iwi, and would build hospitals and schools for them. It should have been an arrangement of mutual benefit – share the land, get access to the benefits of European life. The price in total for more than half the land mass of New Zealand? 14,750 pounds. But even the bargain of the century wasn't quite good enough for the Crown, which reneged on its side of the bargain – no allocation of land, no schools, no hospitals. Ngai Tahu, who had had free range of the South Island, wound up with virtually no land and no resources.

Not that they took it lying down. By 1849, they were petitioning the Crown to set aside adequate reserves as they'd been promised. In 1868, they took the case to the courts, at which point the Government passed laws to prevent the courts from hearing or ruling on the case. A decade later, a commission of inquiry got under way, but the Crown shut down its funding. By the time of the findings on the land claim by the Waitangi Tribunal in 1991, at least a dozen different commissions, inquiries, courts and tribunals had repeatedly established the veracity and justice of the Ngai Tahu claim. When the story was finally told a century and a half later, it became clear: the Crown agents had consistently lied and tricked their away around the South Island to get the land they wanted.

Experiences like this soon made Maori wary, but there were

other reasons as well for not wanting to sell too much: they wanted to be located nearby the growing settlements where they could build their trading links, which had become substantial by the end of the 1840s. They worked for the Government on roading contracts and public works. They supplied the settlements in Auckland and Wellington and, as time went on, other parts of the country as coastal trade built up. They set up hotels, townships and flour mills. The farms they developed had horses, drays, ploughs and other equipment, and grew produce for the markets. The exchange between the cultures was substantial. Auckland shops relied on the trade from Maori and stocked themselves to meet their needs. This was what Maori had been hoping to see when they agreed to the Treaty – the exchange of goods, services and ideas to the mutual benefit of both sides. Naturally, they wanted to remain near the growing communities, so that the relationship could build.

The balance of power at the outset was still substantially in favour of Maori, and they continued to be the larger economic force in the country throughout that first decade. They were the majority in number and they were well armed. The settlers knew their limitations, even if they had their doubts about the Treaty arrangements. They also knew a good deal about those arrangements. The Treaty was regularly discussed in the newspapers and debated in the community.

So in 1846 when the Secretary of State for the Colonial Office, Earl Grey, proposed a scheme that would grant self-government to the settlers – you could vote if you were male and could read and write English – the locals knew it was just asking for trouble. It also proposed that Maori land would have to be registered, with Maori having to prove they owned it and were actively using it. This was a use-it-or-lose-it deal – any land that wasn't registered would be taken by the Crown. It was never going to fly, and Governor Grey knew it. The debate flew round the country and back to London (where it was also debated, with the press writing about the 'humbug Treaty'). In the end, Earl Grey saw he had to climb down and reassure Maori that the Treaty would be honoured and that their land was safe. But for how long?

What we see when we look at this period is very interesting, though. The Treaty is clearly acknowledged to protect the rights of the people living here and it's being used as a guide to the way people should be working together. That's not to say that everything was sweetness and light – the settlers and Maori had differences to be sorted out, and they were by no means dealt with conclusively at that point – but the two sides were finding ways to work together. In many ways, both sides were getting a fair share, and playing a part in the new country that was being built. It gives you a clue as to how things might have turned out if both parties had remained committed to the Treaty. But things were about to change.

If you're looking for the smoking gun in this story, this is the place to look for it. In 1852, power really began shifting from London to New Zealand and into the hands of the settlers. As the settler government took over, and as the number and power of those settlers grew, the gamble that Maori had made really began to work against them. While Britain had a strong influence on policy, there was a conscious commitment to the Treaty, even if it wasn't uniformly supportive or fair in its interpretations, but that waned once the settler governments took over.

What kicked it off was the New Zealand Constitution Act 1852, which gave New Zealand a system of self-government. There were six provincial councils, over which there would be a two-house parliament and an executive council, which in due course would proceed to form its own ministry and Premier, all of which was in motion by 1856. The key question, though, was who could vote for it? Well, anyone who was male and owned property – except communally owned land didn't count, which would have ruled out most otherwise eligible Maori. They qualified to pay tax, however, and were a substantial source of government revenue, and the Act made some effort to safeguard Maori interests in terms of money set aside, and legislation which had to be reserved for Crown assent.

The Wesleyan Missionary Society tried and failed to include a provision that would have effectively had the Treaty ratified by the colonial government. They had an idea that the settler government wouldn't be too concerned with the Treaty or Maori interests and they weren't wrong. The Act was framed with the expectation that Maori could be assimilated – and soon, too – which was the gamble Pakeha had made at the time of the Treaty.

This would be a government composed of characters like Alfred Domett, who admitted that he had 'an utter contempt' for the Treaty, and thought the land guarantee had been 'unwise'. The number of settlers was growing very rapidly. From 2000 or so in 1840 they had reached something near 60,000 by 1860, and the new government was able to call the shots on their behalf. In terms of the Treaty, essentially they charged ahead and acted as though there was an Article I, which gave them sovereignty, but not an Article II, which put important limitations on what that sovereignty meant.

What they especially wanted, of course, was land, and Maori were growing more reluctant to sell. They had seen what had happened when they sold land – accepting low prices for land in return for government promises of schools and hospitals and land reserves that never came, for example, or selling land to one purchaser who they saw as a good prospective trading partner, who would then on-sell – and they were wary of being compromised further. Settlers, meanwhile, were pressing for land and there were more of them arriving every month.

This tension would lead to two crucial points in the history of the colony – the Native Lands Act 1865, and war – both of which would see Maori deprived of vast areas of enormously valuable land.

Maori saw what was happening and wondered if they might not be equally well served by their own system of government, with their own King. They had a point. Governor Browne found when he arrived in 1855 that Maori had no say in the running of things, even though the part they played in the economy was vital. Pakeha authorities were neglecting and ignoring the tribes, and nor were they giving any support to chiefly authority. Not surprisingly, there was support among Maori for some way to unite to protect their land and their rights. Throughout the 1850s, momentum gathered for the idea of rallying behind a Maori King, and in 1858 Potatau Te Wherowhero became the first Maori King, at Ngaruawahia.

Maori supporters of the movement thought the idea sat logically within the Treaty; many settlers saw it as rebellion. It was that issue of kawanatanga versus rangatiratanga again, although it wasn't debated in those terms at a conference that Governor Browne convened at Kohimarama in 1860. He'd called it because he knew he needed to gather Maori support, because a little earlier in the year the prospects for peaceful land settlement had taken a big dive.

In 1859, a Te Ati Awa chief in Taranaki had offered to sell him a piece of land at Waitara. The Governor knew it was risky. Other chiefs who had an interest in the land wouldn't be interested in selling, and the accepted policy was clear enough:

you negotiated with all the interested parties before you went ahead with a deal. But he also knew the settlers expected him to get tough on land sales. They argued that an individual had the right to make his own sale. The Governor took the hard line: he went ahead, forced the sale, and surveyors were sent to peg out the land. Te Ati Awa people challenged them peacefully and disrupted them. The Governor sent in the troops. Fighting broke out, and for the next year there was war in Taranaki.

So now Browne had chiefs gathered from across the North Island at Kohimarama. It effectively became a review of what had happened in 1840. The Governor reinforced some of the undertakings that had been made there: that their rights to forests and fisheries as well as lands were guaranteed. He talked about possession, though, not chieftainship. It emerged that many of those who had signed in 1840 hadn't in fact known exactly what the Treaty's implications would be. Now, however, aware of the implications, they all gave a renewed commitment to it.

From the Governor's point of view, he had their express commitment to the Treaty and to the Queen's sovereignty. What he didn't get from them, though, was any kind of acceptance that a Maori King movement couldn't sit alongside that.

From the point of view of Maori, they had some valuable undertakings from the Governor: they had complained that they weren't given equal participation in law and government. The Governor undertook to make the conference a permanent institution, and promised to reconvene it the following year.

The pity of it was that without an agreement on the King movement, a fight looked inevitable. As time went on, most settlers came to the view that sovereignty was being tested and had to be asserted. Instead of the two parties striking an arrangement that might have shared power and accommodated each side's interests, the settler government had left little room for Maori in the running of things. The outcome would be a confrontation. In May 1861, Browne demanded that the Waikato tribes submit without reserve to the Queen's authority under law.

One of the moderating influences in the King movement, Wiremu Tamihana, wrote back to the Governor, explaining their belief that it was possible, within the terms of the Treaty, for an independent Maori leadership to sit alongside the Queen's sovereignty. The Government took that as a declaration of independence. In November of that year, George Grey returned to become Governor again. He tried to negotiate, but at the same time as he was talking peace, he was constructing a military road from Auckland to the lower Waikato, and a barracks at Kohekohe, inside the King's boundary.

Then in 1863 war broke out again in Taranaki, and it gave Grey an excuse to invade Waikato. Rewi Maniapoto, one of the fierier of the chiefs in the Kingitanga movement, took a fairly inflammatory view of things, and some of his more provocative actions were enough to give Governor Grey the argument that Waikato tribes were threatening Auckland. He sent 700 British troops across the Mangatawhiri Stream into the territory of the Maori King.

We need to look at the bigger picture to understand what was going on here. If you take a drive from Auckland to Wellington, where do you see the richest land? Waikato. In 1863, Maori owned virtually all of it, they were farming it intensively, and it wasn't for sale. So into the picture, with war looming, comes the settler government, with land speculators sitting in more than a few of its seats. And here's the legislation they pass:

> Suppression of Rebellion Act 1863: military courts are established. If you rebel, you may have your lands confiscated.

> You may even face the death penalty. Habeas corpus is suspended – meaning you can be held without trial.
>
> New Zealand Settlements Act 1863: If a 'considerable number' of Maori are believed to be in rebellion, your land can be confiscated.

Whatever you read into the sovereignty question, there's a more important dimension to it; this war was also being fought over land. Over the following year, a number of major battles and minor skirmishes ensued. By its end, more than 1000 Maori and 700 Europeans had died, including women and children at Rangiaowhia whose house of prayer was torched on a Sunday morning. The war had begun because Maori were said to be in rebellion. In fact, they had been invaded, and they were about to pay an enormous price for defending themselves, because now the Government delivered the greatest blow. It declared a vast area of Waikato to be confiscated, taken in punishment for 'rebellion'.

They took all the most fertile land. Maori called the area *raupatu* – land taken in conquest. If you want a guide to government motivation, consider this: the tribe that had been most prominent in the fighting were Ngati Maniapoto. Most of their territory was in rugged hill country. It wasn't taken. On the other hand, tribes in the Waikato who took no part in the fighting, like Ngati Apakura from around Te Awamutu, were expelled from their homes by the troops and became refugees. The dispossessed tribes went south into the King Country, broken.

In total, 1,202,172 acres were seized (although 314,262 were later paid for or returned to Maori who had supported the British). Even more land was confiscated in the Taranaki; Maori on the East Coast lost land in the same way, under the Suppression of Rebellion Act. If you actively or passively resisted surveyors or sales, you were regarded as a rebel and your lands were confiscated. It didn't take much – sometimes nothing more than a suspicion of 'rebellion' was enough.

But there was more to come. Settlers were frustrated that buying Maori land was made more complicated by its communal ownership. Who did you have to negotiate with? Who could speak for everyone? Their solution was to create a short cut to getting freehold title issued. Under the Native Land Act a Land Court was set up. As owner of the land, you would make a claim to the Court, prove you were the owner, and the Court would decide on the basis of the evidence before it who owned the land. You could only sell land to settlers after it had been considered by the Court and the title could carry the names of no more than ten owners approved by the court.

This would have a number of damaging consequences for Maori. Although it made it easier for those Maori who wanted to sell, it did others a lot of harm. If you were the owner and you didn't want to take part in the process, title would automatically vest in the claimant. It was a time-consuming and costly business getting claims surveyed and taking them to court, and ran many into debt. To meet those debts, many had to sell their land. And, of course, it became possible for a minority group to make the sale, take the money and deprive the rest of the owners of their share. The arguments divided Maori communities against themselves and demoralised them. Once again the law was helping the settlers but doing harm, in many cases, to Maori. Thousands of acres were lost in this way.

Through confiscations, shady dealings and laws that worked against the interests of Maori, the 66 million acres they had held in 1840 had dwindled to a small fraction of that by 1890. It's not true to say that every acre they lost was lost through the fault of someone else, but it is certainly true to say that the greater proportion was lost in that way. You lose your land, you lose one of the most substantial economic assets you can have. It was a body blow for Maori and it left them demoralised, disillusioned and pushed to the margin of the economy.

Anne Salmond describes it this way:

> I think people withdrew. For example, people went into the King Country and tried to put up a boundary over which no European would cross. On the East Coast, people withdrew into the heartlands there, but at the same time if you look historically, there were usually Europeans, not so much in the King Country, but certainly on the coast, living amongst those communities. They were usually farming families or traders, later on the people who ran schools, or had the local shop. And so there has never been a complete separation. But it is true to say, I think, that for most European New Zealanders – there was a long period when they didn't have much to do with Maori.

But even in a kind of exile, some Maori would find they were still vulnerable. By the 1870s, Parihaka, in Taranaki, had become the largest Maori village in the country. Dispossessed and disillusioned Maori had come there from around the North Island, led by two figures, Te Whiti O Rongomai and Tohu Kakahi, both committed to non-violence. Their settlement was threatened in 1879 by European settlers occupying previously empty confiscated land. Their response was to plough the fields that were being confiscated. Four hundred ploughmen were arrested and jailed.

The following year, they erected fences across land and roads. More arrests followed, and Parliament legislated to make it possible to hold the protesters without trial. By September 1880, around 150 fencers had been shipped away to the South Island. The Taranaki settlers went on surveying the land and breaking down fences each day, and the villagers went on putting them back up.

The villagers considered they were living in peace, the Government characterised them as dangerous fanatics. On the morning of 5 November 1881, they acted. An invasion force entered Parihaka. More than 2000 villagers sat quietly on the marae as a group of singing children greeted the army. The Riot Act was read and one hour later Te Whiti and Tohu were arrested and led away. The invasion force demolished the village, destroyed the crops and killed the livestock. Some of the Parihaka men were held for up to eighteen years without trial.

That wasn't the end of the story. Parihaka was eventually rebuilt, and Te Whiti and Tohu were finally allowed to return in 1883. But the actions of the Government over that time tell you plenty about their attitude to the Treaty rights of Maori, and their willingness to co-operate with them.

Taranaki saw some of the worst Treaty breaches. Here's what the Waitangi Tribunal would one day have to say about it:

> In most districts, the fighting was over in months, but armed initiatives did not cease in Taranaki until after an unparalleled nine years.
>
> Even then, the period of armed struggle was in fact much longer. History creates time slots to compartmentalise war, and 1860 to 1869 has been given for the Taranaki fighting; but just as conflict was apparent from 1841, so also did it continue after 1869. Military action on the Government's part did not end until the invasion of Parihaka in 1881. Thus, in Taranaki, conflict with the use of arms was spread not over a few months, as in most places, or even over a decade, but over a staggering 40 years. After British sovereignty was proclaimed, in no other part of New Zealand did a contest of that nature continue for so long or Maori suffer so much the deprivations of strife after British sovereignty was proclaimed.
>
> The tension did not cease with the abandonment of arms. The confiscations came with an undertaking that lands necessary for hapu survival would be returned without delay,

> but the promise was not maintained. The same promise was also made in other districts, but we understand that in most cases land was promptly offered and given over for Maori possession. In Taranaki, however, many hapu were left with nothing of their own to live on and became squatters on Crown land. More than a decade after the war, they had not received anything more than promises of land. It was only after more conflict that some reserves were eventually defined, but they were given over to administrators to hold for Maori and 'the promotion of settlement'. They were then leased to settlers on perpetual terms, with the result that Taranaki Maori, and they alone, have still to receive the right to occupy the lands promised after the war.
>
> Legislation is now proposed to terminate those leases within 63 years. Though competing equities now apply, it may none the less be observed that the promises of reserves made in the confiscations of the 1860s, limited though they may have been, have still to be given effect and on current projections will not have final effect for a further 63 years – over 180 years after they were made. It should be seen at once that this history is not a thing of the past.
>
> Thus, the distinctive Taranaki circumstance. If war is the absence of peace, the war has never ended in Taranaki, because that essential prerequisite for peace among peoples, that each should be able to live with dignity on their own lands, is still absent and the protest over land rights continues to be made.

Now, as outrageous as actions like the confiscations and Parihaka and the sly dealing and dispossession were, it outrages some people more than others. Some might say: *Well, you get that kind of thing in history, so what?* This might be an appropriate moment to stop and consider how far things had degenerated in about forty years. Remember that in 1840, Maori outnumbered Pakeha by about thirty to one, and yet they had accepted an arrangement to share power and work together. They expected at the very least a significant role.

Moana Maniapoto puts it well:

> I think it was signed in that view, that there was a relationship ... and there wasn't a war going on, it wasn't a forced situation, there was a lot of good will on the part of Maori because we weren't outnumbered then. So there is no reason why you would cede all your powers and rights to a small bunch of very dodgy-looking characters from overseas.

And as we've seen, for as long as Maori had the greater armed power, people kept the Treaty largely in their consideration. But gradually, as more settlers arrived, the balance changed, and as it did, regard for the Treaty withered. If you think, as many settlers came to, that things would be better if there had never been a Treaty, then the best day of the nineteenth century for you was probably in 1877 when the Chief Justice, Sir James Prendergast, ruled that the Treaty was:

> 'worthless – a simple nullity [which] pretended to be an agreement between two nations but [in reality] was between a civilised nation and a group of savages ...'

It was in that spirit that the nineteenth century saw the settler government pulling all the blankets over to its side of the bed. Once the wars were over, any ideas of sharing or mutual benefit were put out of mind. The talk was much plainer: *We're in charge, and you'd better toe the line.* Here's a sample:

> The Maori Representation Act 1867: set up four Maori seats as a means of removing the threat of Maori outnumbering Pakeha in some electorates where individualised titles had given Maori the right to vote. Maori men could only vote in these four seats.
>
> The Maori Prisoners' Trials Act 1879: trials were postponed and finally dispensed with for Maori accused of hindering surveying of land. And just to underline how little they were worried

> about the rights of a British subject under Article III of the Treaty, they also suspended habeas corpus.
>
> The Native Land Purchase and Acquisition Act 1893: reintroduced the Crown right of pre-emption. The Crown was given new powers to declare any Maori land 'suitable for settlement'. When they resisted, Maori found themselves facing armed troops once more.
>
> The Crown and Native Lands Rating Act 1882: Maori land within five miles of a highway was made liable to rates. The Crown paid the rates to the local body and made the debt a first charge on the land. That debt quite often led to land having to be sold.

The worst of all this for Maori was that there seemed to be nowhere to find a remedy. They sent petitions to Parliament – hundreds of them. They tried the courts, but the Treaty wasn't recognised. They convened a Maori Parliament, but the Parliament in Wellington didn't recognise it. They petitioned the Queen, asking her to investigate and rectify laws that contravened the Treaty. They told her of the confiscations, the Native Land Court, Parihaka, and a long list of Acts that acted against the principles contained in the Treaty. Her Majesty was unable to assist.

There were of course four Maori Members of Parliament also making their protests, but they couldn't get a response from the majority of the members. If you dust off a copy of Hansard or two, you'll find it all there, year after year. Attorney-General Margaret Wilson sees that as particularly significant.

> Representation of Maori in Parliament was extraordinarily important, because that kept a visibility – this is just my view – but it seemed it kept a visibility and an acknowledgement that that there were issues unaddressed. And that enabled generation after generation of Maori politicians . . . their job was

to never let anybody forget. And they didn't. It was expressed in a variety of different ways.

Treaty grievance and protest by Maori are nothing new. They were knocking on the door more than 100 years ago, ever since the grievances arose. But for the longest time, the knock went unanswered.

'This Maori Identity stuff is crap. We're all New Zealanders.'

WHEN THINGS reach the point that officials in the government are using an expression like 'smooth the pillow of a dying race' it's clear that things have come to a pretty desperate turn. It wasn't, as anyone who was at Waitangi in 1840 would have told you, supposed to be turning out that way.

Let's think about the larger picture for a moment, because it goes a long way to explaining why we've ended up with the debate we're having. The Treaty was supposed to do what Lord Normanby indicated in as many words: protect the interests of the indigenous people. The settlers had been so hell-bent on getting land that their obligations under the Treaty were pushed aside and ignored, and Maori ended up precisely in the position Normanby had said they should never be: deprived of their land, disillusioned and to a large degree exiled to the margins of life in New Zealand.

Land had given them economic strength and identity, now they had little of either. Their common interests in traditional lands had held them together and given them a common purpose. That purpose was gone now for many Maori. The people who had been so active in the economy and strong in their own culture, who had been enthusiastically absorbing and swapping with European culture had been completely derailed. The opportunity to develop and work together, which is what the Treaty contemplated, had gone. Communities had broken up, many were living in the most basic of circumstances, and for a good number of them the spirit and purpose had gone out of their life. And if losing their land wasn't sufficient to ruin their lives, there were also the effects of disease to contend with. By 1890 the Maori population had declined to less than forty-three thousand.

The Pakeha perspective shifted. Where once the expectation had been that Maori might be absorbed into settler society and become brown Pakeha, the thought towards the end of the nineteenth century was that Maori seemed likely to die out altogether. But, of course, the story turned in a different direction.

Margaret Wilson puts it this way:

> They were a people who were defeated, in large part, and they were defeated in battle, but the main defeat was of course the confiscation of land. Your place, which you always thought was yours, was suddenly taken away from you. That meant that on top of everything else that was happening with colonisation in effect you had a whole culture that had to go into retreat for survival. And it did go into retreat for survival to the areas that were left to it, while the rest of the society sort of got on – and took advantage of it and prospered on the confiscated land and prospered on the rest of the land without really having to account for all the consequences of that.

The way back came through a revival of mana, of purpose, of identity, and the prospect of a future. It was delivered in part by a number of extremely talented men, most of whom were students at Te Aute College. They had a message of survival for their people: Maori could recover. It was a message they began to deliver while they were still in school, travelling during their holidays to the small communities around the country. They talked about ways of improving life for Maori – education, ventilated housing, agriculture, economic development and health and hygiene. They told them the way forward would be to adapt to Western society, but to retain a strong Maori cultural identity.

They would become the Young Maori Party, and they would lead a social, economic and cultural revival. Maui Pomare and Peter Buck became medical graduates and went into politics. Apirana Ngata, who qualified first in law, became an MP in 1905 and over the next forty years he guided a programme for recovery that was both cultural and economic. He championed loan schemes that would allow money to be advanced to Maori to develop farms. He also encouraged Maori to recover the old skills – carving, haka, oral culture. Around the country, they revived their culture. They built meeting houses. They held hui. The culture began to flower again. And at the same time Maori brought land back into production and built up successful farms.

Many tribal leaders picked up the lead and began their own cultural revivals – like Te Puea Herangi of Tainui for example. The result was profound: identity began to take shape and grow, and divided communities began to find unity again. Health improved and the population began to increase.

Meanwhile, the Government was acting in new, but not necessarily more helpful, ways. The Maori Councils Act 1900 set up local Maori committees, but they were given little real power. Ngata wanted Government to encourage a strong Maori identity but that was not only sidelined in legislation but in one way or another was actively discouraged. Maori children couldn't speak Maori in the school grounds, and were punished if they did. Maori adoption practices were all but prohibited. Yes, the initiatives that came with the Welfare State included Maori, but policy continued to be shaped from a Pakeha point of view.

The Young Maori philosophy wasn't the only one to win support among Maori, though. The Ratana movement began with the ideas of one charismatic man and grew from a faith-healing beginning to become a potent political force, advocating statutory ratification of the Treaty.

These changes had a profound impact, but there were bigger ones to come. At the beginning of the Second World War, less than one in nine Maori lived in urban areas. By the end, a quarter were there, and within a generation the great majority had moved away from the rural areas. The instinct to stay close to your own land and family and marae had kept Maori in the country, but that changed for a number of reasons.

Work was becoming available in the towns – manual work, at good pay, in labouring, construction, meat plants. At the same time, in their traditional homes, the population was growing, and although the farms that had been developed were doing well, they couldn't carry the weight of those new numbers. Add to that the experience of the young men who had come back home after fighting in the Maori Battalion. They had a new perspective and new plans, and weren't necessarily going to adhere to the old ways.

But adapting to the new urban life was another thing. And this would be the point at which an old myth would start to look a bit shaky: New Zealand with its harmonious race relations enjoyed that harmony largely because the two races had not had a great deal to do with each other for many decades, and one of them had been in retreat. Now they were living in the same streets, going to the same schools, and drinking in the same pubs, and it started to become apparent that there were differences and divisions there.

Identity is one of those words that can make a good honest Kiwi squirm a bit – *Don't know what you're on about, mate.* But that doesn't mean it doesn't amount to something quite important, even if we don't know how to put it into words. TV interviewer Kim Hill asked Opposition Leader Don Brash, not long after his Orewa speech, what it meant to him to be a New Zealander. He was a bit unsure about that. But as he tried to work out what that was, one thing was clear: he knew he felt he belonged in New Zealand and that there was a place for him. (Not that everyone might have agreed at the time; but I digress.)

Identity, in part, is the feeling that you belong, that there's a place for you, that somehow you have a role to play. For some Maori who were now living in the towns and cities, that feeling didn't come so readily. They were getting the feeling that they didn't exactly fit, that there wasn't really a place for them. Maori started to see that they were not the same as these other people, and they weren't always treated in the same way. At the same time, their own ties with the whanau and marae were being broken. Children were growing up with no connection to that life and that culture, and it left them confused. They didn't entirely fit into the Pakeha world, but their own one was back somewhere else, and they didn't know all that much about it.

Not all Maori were growing up in that way, of course. Shane Jones is today the Chairman of Te Ohu Kai Moana, the Maori Fisheries Commission, and his career has taken him through many of the key moments in the fight for Maori rights.

He remembers the instruction he grew up with:

> I went to St Stephens School for five years and I don't actually remember being taught about the Treaty at school. We certainly got taught a lot about our culture. And I had the good fortune to have a grandmother and come from a community where Maori things were talked about a lot, especially by my old people. They hoped that I would become a clergyman, as was the trajectory for a lot of people with promise in small Maori communities. And of course that never happened for me, but they began to develop me and to ensure that I could speak Maori and had appropriate respect, I suppose, for the customs of the marae and in particular oratory.

He agrees, though, that Maori who had joined that urban drift were being pulled into a different system that thought it would be best if they left their Maori identity behind.

> ... you think back to ... the early 1960s, there probably was a view that if we move Maori to the cities they would be a pool of blue-collar workers because they already were in many cases hewers of wood and carriers of water.
>
> In moving them to the cities, the churches had some influence over them and a number of them created urban marae. But when you think of the scale of the population those were really faint brown dots of hope, really, in relation to identity and heritage.
>
> And I should imagine that people thought the Maori, once they moved into metropolitan New Zealand, would be absorbed into the sort of amorphous Kiwi ethic. And what is fascinating is that since the 1970s the whole concept of identity itself has become political to the Maori.

The great pity of it was that a lot of momentum was going to be interrupted. Maori had been recovering. The sense of purpose and sense of identity that had been developing was looking vulnerable again. Many Maori would find that the better life in the towns wasn't necessarily going to stay better. For the first decade or two after the war ended, full employment made it fine. But then the economy turned south, and unskilled, well-paying jobs weren't so easy to find. That fed into a poverty cycle – lower standards of housing and health, higher rates of crime, reducing prospects of finding jobs – leading to lower standards of housing and health and … you get the picture. There were going to be problems.

TEST YOUR TREATY KNOWLEDGE 5

How many Treaty claims have been settled?

A. 1
B. 5
C. 10
D. 12
E. 15

(Answers page 199)

CHAPTER SIX: RESISTANCE

'The Treaty is a fraud.'

GOVERNMENTS NEVER like getting bad news, and the Hunn Report in 1960 was a document of that kind. It offered a picture of the state of Maori in New Zealand, and it made it pretty clear that the statistics weren't good. The disparity between Maori and Pakeha was clear to see, and it was obvious that the drift of Maori to the towns and cities wasn't going well. If, like Don Brash, you don't like the idea of ethnicity-based funding, then you wouldn't have liked the remedies that followed the Hunn Report all that much, even though it had a different aim. The prescription was essentially: *If you blend the two cultures, the problems will go away.*

But Maori were looking at their new circumstances and concluding that blending wasn't anything like the right answer. The break with their roots was eroding their language and their culture. They didn't have the whanau, they didn't have the marae, which meant that many of them didn't have the language being taught and were losing touch with their culture. Well, that's no problem, right? Don't you pick up the culture of the place you've moved to? There was certainly a Pakeha point of view that saw it that way – *Never mind what you've left behind, fill the gap with our culture.*

But if you were a young Maori, you noticed that the culture didn't entirely make room for you. It seemed, at times, to work a little better for the Pakeha than it did for you, and it had a habit of pointing out to you that you weren't entirely part of it. If you wanted to explore your Maori culture, where did you go? Back to the village on the coast? That probably wasn't the way Sir Apirana Ngata hoped it would be.

All of this was exercising a new generation of Maori who would come to be much more active and vocal about their concerns. They were asking themselves: *Why are so many of our people poor? Why don't they have skilled jobs? Why are our young people getting in trouble?* They watched Maori dropping into a poverty cycle, they saw how Maori were drifting to the edges of the economy, and they saw that Maori language and culture were being lost by many urban Maori.

As they looked at the problem, and asked the questions, and looked back at the history, they came to the view that this was no accident, and it was by no means some inherent fault on the part of Maori. Much of the property and power that Maori once had was gone, and there was a reason for that. Maori had been short-changed; often, and over a very long stretch of time. It was time, they thought, to put that right.

They were educated, they were aware of what was going on elsewhere in the world with indigenous people agitating for their rights, and they knew how to argue their case strongly and get attention. Initially, their concern was with getting Maori culture and identity known and accepted in the Pakeha world. They argued that it was a Treaty right and that it should be honoured. But the argument evolved.

The Young Maori Party had taken the view that you could

have a foot in both camps – live like a Pakeha, think like a Maori. Activists in this new generation came to see things differently as they explored the ideas of indigenous rights and the rights the Treaty was supposed to have given Maori. They thought that a foot in both camps would just put you back in the situation you'd been in in the nineteenth century, and that hadn't worked. They thought the answer to the problems Maori had inherited was to reclaim what was guaranteed under the Treaty: Maori sovereignty – rangatiratanga.

So on top of the arguments they had been making to bring Maori language and culture into the light, they now added another: *Give Maori some ownership and control.* They wanted Maori autonomy and Maori authority, and if Pakeha didn't like it they could take their colonising ways and go home. Well, of course, that went down a treat.

Shane Jones was there for a lot of the fun, a veteran of the reborn Maori protest movement, with a tradition of making marches to Waitangi.

> As I look back there were really two dimensions to it. There was a dimension of political nationalism, and cultural nationalism, the latter being relearning language, halting the erosion of our heritage and identity, and political nationalism really bringing the tactics of political protest politics to bear – trying to effect changes in the minds and attitudes of the state, ministers and indeed our own people.
>
> Some of the staunchest figures, people like Hana Jackson, Syd Jackson, Ti Harawera, were obviously Maori, but they were a proxy for a whole bunch of people who had become dislocated. And we were slightly different in that we came from rural New Zealand. Some of my other cousins had come back from Australia. They immediately spotted that dislocation, so those of us in the North we were a mix. Some of us had come from families that were very, very much intact, into marae life, into Anglican Church life. Others were from an urban

experience, South Auckland, and others were looking for their own identity and they were drawn to those manifestations of renaissance which was the protest movement.

And as time went on, I moved into contact with people who probably were a bit more structured and certainly from the more conservative end of the Maori spectrum, namely Sir Graham Latimer, Matiu Rata. Both those kamautua came from my area, and I'd fallen under the tutelage of Reverend Maori Marsden, and he was a clergyman with a radical perspective on things and a great Maori scholar. I moved to Wellington after concluding that the things I wanted to do with my life couldn't be fully achieved through the protest movement.

Support for this movement came from other groups as well as Maori, as Margaret Wilson points out:

There has always been a link and a thread in New Zealand society that acknowledges and respects the legitimacy of the position of Maori and of the Treaty. And that link has come in a variety of ways. It came though Labour, because it was an identification with working-class people and impoverishment. That's who Labour represented. Maori were a large proportion of the population who were impoverished, and outside the system. So it was that social justice link that actually brought the peoples together.

I haven't actually seen this fully explored, but I think that was extremely important, because the renaissance that came in the late 1960s and '70s couldn't have come unless there was a sympathetic platform, and also intellectually, in New Zealand, a willingness to see the justice of the cause, because most of the social movements in the '60s and the '70s embraced the renaissance of Maori as a good thing and as something that should be addressed in those inequalities.

Now, that didn't come from nowhere. And it wasn't only imported as part of a civil rights movement from the US ... When you went back, the stories of European New Zealanders that had objected to apartheid and the racially divided [rugby]

> teams that went to South Africa were much further back than most people thought. There had always been this thread that could be called upon – the strand from the settlers that respected and acknowledged that justice had to be done to Maori.

For a great many people though, this was all news – and a bit of a shock. Cabinet Minister and urban Maori advocate John Tamihere believes it was inevitable that it would be a surprise, given how little most of us had learned about our own history.

> Our education system was fully English-based. Only other language, French. Tudor England, Reformation – all those sorts of things. That was predicated on the huge umbilical cord we had with Great Britain until about 1973 when it chose to go to the EEC. And we only started to wake up to ourselves and our place then. And up until that time, what we got was a Morrie Minor, Morrie 1100, Morrie 1300 stepping up to a Zephyr maybe, or a Vauxhall, then maybe if you got there a Rover, maybe a Jag, but that was it, and everything was English. And we never had to think about ourselves. Our benchmarks were all given to us from Shakespeare all the way through. We did not honour and respect our own literary artists even. So we just did not have a sense of nation properly.
>
> And in fact you had Michael Joseph Savage declaring war on Germany nine hours before Britain did, saying, 'Where Britain goes, we go. Where she stands, we stand.' And there was a surge of patriotism for the motherland. See, my own mother, third-generation Pakeha, often talked about the old country.
>
> So this is a very recent thing. Post-Second World War there was not a Maori story. The Young Maori Party died off, with Ratana taking over the seats. He put in people who were not necessarily quick and clever, but out in the communities, he was charismatic. It wasn't until the late 1950s when you see Ranginui Walker and all the rest of them coming through.
>
> All of a sudden we have to define who *we* are. We got the first oil shocks and we've got the formation of the Waitangi Tribunal

> in 1975, which nobody knew anything about. It was one of the last pieces of legislation of the outgoing Rowling government – first application of it was taken by Joe Hawke as Rowling was getting bundled out in 1978. And in fact 1978 was the first time a lot of Pakeha New Zealand woke up to the fact that there were some Maori grievances around on the basis of Bastion Point. It wasn't about Ngati Whatua; it was a rallying point for all Maori.

As the debate gathered pace, Pakeha academics began going back for another look. They offered some new perspectives on a history that had been taken for granted – with the surprising news for many that the Treaty had been far from honoured.

Elsewhere, of course, this came as less of a shock, as Shane Jones explains:

> A brief appraisal of the history of the Ratana church would show that Ratana had two taonga that he offered Maori: one was the Bible and the other was the Treaty of Waitangi. And if you read [JM] Henderson's book on Ratana the prophet, it recounts a fantastic story where Aperahama Taonui, the Ngapuhi prophet at the time the Treaty was signed, counselled his own people not to sign the Treaty if it meant that it would be cloaked with the Union Jack. It was a figurative way of saying, 'cloak it with the Kiwi feather cloak' – if it envelops us with the Union Jack we will be sad that you ever did that ...
>
> So Ratana picked up on that and wandered around the country accentuating the connection between the Bible and the Treaty, in that the Treaty was consummated in the presence of the missionaries. And that the Treaty was marked with the moko, which would have been a very tapu sign. Marked with the moko of the ancestors. And the way in which Maori talked about it was that it was written in their blood. It had all the parallels of an allegory: a very symbolic thing ...
>
> Then after that you find that certain people in Ngapuhi, in particular Sir James Henare and his tribe, they were very, very insistent about maintaining the connection with the Treaty. I don't know much about the Ngai Tahu, but I know they had a

> tradition down there of trying to get their land back, and Sir Tipene's spoken about that at length. In relation to the Tainui, they had the history of the raupatu. I'm not sure whether they conceived that raupatu history through the prism of the Treaty or whether it was looked at through their shabby treatment after the land wars.
>
> So it would be incorrect to say that there was a blanket indifference to the Treaty among Maori. There were pockets of people who remembered it, who talked about it, who used it to keep certain traditions alive. But it's not an unreasonable thing to say that once Maori moved en masse to the cities . . . there was a bout of economic prosperity and it really took the protest groups of the late '60s and early '70s to awaken Maori in general. And that was a long process, and indeed some of the most fierce critics of the original protestors were the kaumatua themselves.

Change came gradually. But that's not to say that governments of both stripes weren't making moves to respond, as the mood for a rebalancing of the scales grew. They came to see they would have to take a bicultural approach. You didn't just try to look after Maori by assimilating them – you gave them their own room to stand. This saw the beginning of Kohanga Reo – the language nests that would teach the language to new generations of Maori. The Race Relations Act 1971 passed, which played no small role in getting people to reconsider the way they spoke of, thought of and treated Maori. And in 1975 there came the establishment of the Waitangi Tribunal.

Pakeha had more or less forgotten about the Treaty; Maori never had. In 1975, Matiu Rata had a bill before Parliament proposing that a tribunal be set up to enquire into claims from Maori that they had been prejudicially affected by any action or omission of the Crown which they believed to be inconsistent with the principles of the Treaty of Waitangi. It would only apply to something that had happened after the Act was passed, so its scope was by no means wide.

Cabinet wasn't all that sure about it, but out on State Highway One the Land March of 1975 was working its way from the top of the North Island, across the Auckland Harbour Bridge and all the way to Parliament grounds. It was a vast show of solidarity and it was a reminder to the Government that, compared to the alternatives, this might be a prudent way to deal with the grievances being raised. The Treaty of Waitangi Act became law at the end of 1975.

Even though the Tribunal was small and had limited scope, it would prove to have quite an influence on thinking about the Treaty over the next few years. That became especially clear in 1983 when it delivered its findings in the Motunui claim. Te Ati Awa claimed that a sewage outfall at Waitara had destroyed their traditional fishing grounds, and a new outfall for industrial waste at Motunui threatened to have the same effect. The Crown had let this discharge take place, destroying their resources. It was a breach of the Treaty, the tribe said. The Tribunal agreed, and the way in which it reached its decision gave everyone some idea of what the Treaty meant, and how it might be relevant to current-day circumstances.

For one thing, it recognised the importance of spiritual and cultural values associated with fisheries. It said that the traditional rights and values might sometimes have a privileged place in planning decisions – not just one more factor to be weighed up when a decision was being made.

It also recognised that it was important to include the present-day reality of a situation, so that a compromise solution might see Maori interests protected, but in a way that avoided imposing fresh injustice on someone else.

It also offered some guidance about interpreting the Treaty – it said you should be looking to the principles, rather than the precise wording, to find a way to get a result that was fair to everyone in the current-day circumstances. That thinking would have a significant influence in the coming years.

But there were still much larger questions that had come back on the agenda. What about the enormous loss that Maori had suffered when all that land had been taken? There had been settlements of sorts made in the 1920s and 1940s, but nothing sufficient to genuinely deal with the grievances and the harm that had been done. And what about this question of rangatiratanga versus sovereignty? What about the rights of Maori to have a say in the running of the country? What was going to be done about that?

It would present governments with a dilemma: how to balance the expectations of Maori against the response of the rest of the voters. For every voter who was enthusiastic and supportive – bone carving around the neck and practising what Winston Peters used to like to call 'sickly white liberalism' – you'd find one who was outraged. Somewhere in the middle sat broad public opinion.

Governments responded over time by making changes to satisfy agitation without necessarily selling them to people who didn't want to hear. The result was a disconnection between those *within* the system – government, bureaucracy, political parties, protestors, media, who would be well-acquainted with the issues – and those *outside*, the general public, who weren't.

This was the backdrop to issues like the Land March in 1975 and the occupation of Bastion Point in the late 1970s. As much as the Government had moved forward, activists could see there was a lot more still to be argued for. The headlines got angrier – *Kill a White*, *Students at Haka Practice Bashed*, *Angry Scenes at Waitangi* – and as the 1980s rolled on, the tension kept building.

TEST YOUR TREATY KNOWLEDGE 6

How many Treaty claims have been heard by the Waitangi Tribunal and are approaching settlement?

A. 1
B. 5
C. 10
D. 12
E. 15

(Answers page 199)

CHAPTER SEVEN: BACK TO THE FUTURE

'It was 160 years ago. Why are we digging all this up now?'

> I have said that the Treaty of Waitangi has the potential to be our nation's most powerful unifying symbol. I trust that these principles demonstrate that there is a place for all New Zealanders within the Treaty of Waitangi.
>
> DAVID LANGE

ONE WINTER night in 1984, the Prime Minister emerged from his office after an evening of gin and arguments and tried one last throw of the political dice. He called a snap election, and lost. It came a little sooner than the Labour Party had been expecting, so the economic policy in their manifesto might not have predicted what would happen as well as it might have. On the other hand, the manifesto was quite clear on one thing: they proposed to widen the scope of the Waitangi Tribunal.

That policy would have an effect every bit as significant, in its own way, as Rogernomics. The big Treaty settlements seen over the last few years would not have been possible without that change, and if you believe the country *has* gone overboard with PC gestures to Maori in the last decade or so, then, in a less direct way, that policy might be one place to put some of the blame. But there's a little more to it than just changes to the Waitangi Tribunal.

First things first: how did the policy come to be in the manifesto? Sir Geoffrey Palmer was in charge of the Labour Party policy council at the time. He explains why they thought the Tribunal should have its jurisdiction extended back to 1840.

> If you were going to look at doing justice effectively, you had to deal with the historical grievances, because they were real, and they weren't going to go away, and they did need to be addressed. And that was a very radical policy in its day. But it was put through the Parliament relatively effectively and it was implemented. Now, of course, quite a lot of the historical grievances have been dealt with, but you couldn't deal with any until 1986.
>
> Effectively it had been ignored, that's the truth of it, up until 1975. The Tribunal was then very scantly resourced and it didn't have much work to do because it only had prospective jurisdiction. The thing that impressed me most about the Tribunal was the Motunui outfall decision they did. I was very interested in that. I was in the Parliament by then, and I thought the way they handled that was pretty good. I mean, it was dealing with real issues that had real Maori cultural significance. And I felt that a tribunal that could handle that in that way was probably worth having its jurisdiction extended back to dealing with the historical grievances, because without dealing with the historical grievances, you were never going to get quiescence. Never.

Was there strong lobbying for this within the party?

> I think the Maori segment of the party thought it was a pretty good idea. [Maori Affairs Minister] Koro Wetere certainly did. I don't think you'd say it was overwhelming though.

Outside the party, of course, there were a lot of people who had been waiting a long time for something like this. It was a chance for the justice Maori had been looking for. Ngai Tahu's Sir Tipene O'Regan says it changed the political climate overnight.

> It was really unavoidable, but it's amazing how fast people have forgotten the enormous civil disturbance, pain and misery that was starting to become very manifest in society, and a fair measure of violence as well starting to show up.
>
> And things were getting uglier and uglier and almost overnight with the passage of that Act, calm descended and people turned themselves to the business of due process. And it was almost like lancing a boil.
>
> But that action at that time, you had the combination of political protest and grievance and . . . that protest base through the 1970s was remarkable. Across all income groups – leadership and what people call radical elements, students and so on. The thing was absolutely cluttered with everything from doctors to archbishops to highly achieving conservative people. And the most rabid student radical wasn't saying anything much different from what Sir James Henare was saying.
>
> Resentment was respectable in the Maori world in that phase. And that was defused and I think, politically, it was of huge importance. It is now looked upon by a lot of journalists and members of the *commentariat* as something of a negative point, but if society had not done it then, we might have well had a very different outcome over the balance of the century . . . You've only just got to get a couple of stupid actions. You just need another Bastion Point or a few things like that and you would have had a really significant strain.

So what was it about this decision that persuaded people to calm down? It was because, for the first time, they were offered the prospect of getting the justice they had long sought.

The Government passed the Waitangi Tribunal Amendment

Act 1985 and declared that the Waitangi Tribunal could investigate claims back to 1840 when the Treaty was signed. It would be an understatement to say the Tribunal could expect to be busy. It was given more resources, more members and a research team.

The task remained the same as it had been when the Tribunal was set up in 1975: to hear claims from Maori who felt that, firstly, an act or omission of the Crown had prejudicially affected them, and secondly, that the act or omission was inconsistent with the principles of the Treaty of Waitangi. The Tribunal could inquire into the claim, make findings and, if it thought the claim was well founded, make recommendations to the government on steps they might take.

Maori who had been arguing for as long as 140 years that their Treaty rights had been denied would have their day in court. They would have the chance to show that, for example, the Crown might not have kept its side of the deal when a sale was made – breaking a promise to build schools or set aside reserves, for instance. If the Crown had declared it had bought land that iwi didn't believe they had sold, or if it had bought it from someone who didn't have the right to sell it, they could seek redress. If their land had been confiscated after the Land Wars or if it had been taken for public works but not used for that purpose, they would finally have somewhere to make their claim. And if their fishing rights hadn't been protected or access to burial grounds and other sacred sites hadn't been respected, that grievance could now be heard.

Not everyone thought this was such a terrific idea. *It'll cost a fortune*, they said. *This will divert attention from their real problems. That's what we should be worrying about. We'll be opening old wounds; what good will that do?*

It would be better to look ahead, they argued, and *just get on with it.*

But sometimes you can't just get on with it. Just because the Crown never answered the door, doesn't mean that Maori didn't have a right to keep knocking. If you have rights under the law and the Crown ignores them, what do you do? You could resort to violence – it's happened elsewhere. On the other hand, you could just keep plugging away, asking for your day in court, hoping that one day you'll get it. Maori chose the non-violent option, and waited several lifetimes for that day to come. Sir Tipene O'Regan reminded us that some people might not have been able to go on waiting much longer.

We know what happened to Ngati Whatua, we know about Tainui and Ngati Awa, we know about the confiscations, we know about Parihaka, we know how Ngai Tahu were swindled – the stories are real, and the people of those iwi did not forget. What the Crown had done, and failed to do, was wrong.

But it was all so long ago. Those people are dead and gone. What's the point in going back to it now?

Matthew Palmer is Dean of Law at Victoria University. He was involved in the negotiations for the Tainui Treaty settlements and he looks at it this way:

> If you look at any set of relationships, if there is some action which has occurred in the past between people in a relationship that is a significant disjuncture, it really causes a breakdown in the relationship. You actually can't make much forward progress.
>
> You've actually got to go back and say, 'We realise that there was a wrong done here' – if there was – 'and we're sorry, we're going to do what we can to make it up,' and if there's actually a real reconciliation there, an addressing of that historical grievance, then that provides the basis on which you can go forward in the relationship.

> So that's why the historical settlements are important, because you can't actually make forward progress otherwise. And if you look at Ngai Tahu for example – Tainui's another example, but in a different way – but with Ngai Tahu the relationships are going ahead in a way which they weren't before the settlements.

We know that Maori started with 66 million acres of land in 1840 and ended up with most of it gone. We know that a large proportion of that land was taken from them against their will, or unjustly. Let's ask a simple question: If they hadn't lost it, do you think they would be better off today? And given that you just said yes, is it not fair to do at least something to reinstate them to the position they would otherwise have been in? (As it happens, the reinstatements so far don't come anywhere near the true value, but we'll get to that.)

Another way of looking at it: a deal is a deal and the law is the law. If that had happened to your family, would you give up without a fight? Now, you might say that something not unlike this happened to your ancestors in Scotland. The thing is, that really is another argument. We're not there, we're here. And here, we have a specific treaty that says the indigenous people have rights.

Maybe you prefer the view that says *There was a war, they lost, get over it*. Tom Bennion, who edits the *Maori Law Review*, knows his way around these issues very well. He worked in the Waitangi Tribunal and these days practises as a barrister.

> One argument is that of Jock Brookfield – this is New Zealand's foremost constitutional scholar – who's saying if you read the Treaty, it's extremely clear: that just on a logical basis Maori could not have given Parliament parliamentary sovereignty in an absolute sense, because if Maori had done that, they would have understood that absolute sovereignty meant that Parliament could have legislated away the very things it was

> guaranteeing. So logically they wouldn't have done it. So parliamentary sovereignty, from the point of view of Maori, even if they'd understood the full concept of parliamentary sovereignty, must have been limited. Parliament has acted as if it wasn't limited and it has done things like pass confiscation legislation, so there is a historical illegitimacy in the New Zealand constitution – this is from New Zealand's foremost constitutional scholar.
>
> So he says, 'What's the remedy for that? If at the base of the unwritten constitution there's a problem, there's an obvious logical injustice, that's irrefutable, what do you do?' And he just says, basically, he can cite hundreds of historical examples where time heals. That is, there is a present Government in force that may have come into force, you could say, by revolution, because it broke those constitutional guarantees, but no one's challenging it and there are hundreds of examples where you don't challenge the current government, it just gets legitimacy over time. And he says, look, one of those aspects of that legitimacy over time is the Waitangi Tribunal. The current government can increase its legitimacy by saying, 'Not only are we in power and we run the armed forces' – it's a crude argument but it holds good constitutionally – 'but also we have certain mechanisms to deal with the past.' So that's a constitutional scholar's view.

Let's say you don't buy any of this. Let's say that as far as you can see, the Treaty just doesn't stand up – either because the parties didn't understand what they were signing, or because the British ended up running the show by force, or any reason you like. Sorry – doesn't actually get you a free pass. It's those lawyers and academics again. If there hadn't been a treaty, then the doctrine of aboriginal title would have been everything. (Actually, before you look at the doctrine, it would also pay to ask yourself this: how far do you suppose the British, or any other nation that fancied colonising the place might have got without getting a pretty fair sort of a fight? But leaving aside that fairly big 'what if', let's look at the law.) Remember the *Mabo* case in Australia? You'd have had cases just like that here. We New Zealanders haven't got this on our own. There are a number of legal systems like ours, particularly those of the United States, Canada and Australia, which have had to look at the problems of indigenous peoples.

What comes through loud and clear – if you take a look at the issue – is that indigenous peoples are entitled to fair treatment by common law and by international law. You can't ignore them, they won't let you, and really, when they've been treated badly, why exactly should they?

Margaret Wilson puts it this way:

> What happens is that people have an identity which they will express regardless. Now in a democratic society, which we have, there is a right to express that identity and it's a right that's expressed universally and it's a right that's expressed in New Zealand. To say this is all in the past and it doesn't count today for me – it's a denial of reality because if I feel I have a grievance, and the evidence supports that, then I have a grievance and telling me to get over it and move on isn't necessarily going to do the trick.
>
> Now you can get to the next stage, where you say *right*, as we have done in New Zealand – which is quite unique – we have collectively decided we will acknowledge legitimate grievance where it actually happened, based on evidence, and then we'll move on. Now the question and the real test of this is whether we do move on. And that, I suppose, really, we cannot determine for some years to come. But the whole basis of doing this is to enable people to move on. Because if there's stuff unresolved in the past then you just go on relitigating it ... Look at Europe, look at Africa, look at, well, even look at the United States now, with the actions being brought by the Black American community suing for slavery. So it's a denial of reality. It just is. You can sort of put your head in the sand, but it's not going to go away.

> What I guess we've been trying to do, in a way, is say: we don't want to embed grievance in our history. We want to deal with it early in our history while we're still close enough to it that we can, and some of the evidence that we're taking now is that at the end of the nineteenth century, beginning of the twentieth century in terms of use of Maori land. So it's sort of almost in living memory or a generation away from it. I mean, it's close to us. We can therefore deal with it on as good evidence as you can so it's not shrouded in too much myth. Whereas if you leave these grievances for generations after generations after generations, the embedding becomes so great that I don't know how you deal with it as, of course, Europe tells us.

There is also the simple justice of it: Maori have been wronged, and they deserve to have that injustice put right. If you take a more pragmatic view of things, and like to see us *just get on with it*, there's one more argument to consider. Treaty settlements have the potential to fix a present problem. If you don't like the look of the unemployment rate, or the number of Maori on welfare, or the number of Maori in trouble with the law, you might at least hope that some settlement money might help turn things around. We'll look at that in a little more depth shortly.

At the end of 1985, the Treaty of Waitangi Amendment Act was passed. Hunter's law applied. Nothing happened overnight, but it did happen. In the next chapter, we'll look at the way things developed once the Tribunal began to investigate those claims, but before we do, we need to look at one other very important step the new government took.

An important part of Rogernomics was the State-Owned Enterprises Act 1986. Under that Act, various government departments were going to be put on a more businesslike footing. They'd run at a profit or loss, and trade in the same way as private companies. As part of that process, the SOE Act would transfer Crown lands to these new entities. In it, section 27 of the Act said that if you'd laid a claim with the Waitangi Tribunal over land which was affected by the Act, it would still be subject to that claim. In addition, section 9 said something altogether broader. Sir Geoffrey Palmer explains it:

> [That] arose quite quickly and quite specifically as a result of representation we had from Sir Hepi Te Heu Heu and others who said, 'Look, all this land is going out of the Crown and into the SOEs and we may have claims against it and how the hell are we ever going to have them satisfied now? And we really don't think that you should be able to do this contrary to the Treaty.'
>
> And Colin Keating – who was helping me with the SOE Act at that time – and I sat down and looked at that, and we thought, 'Well it wouldn't do any harm to put in a provision in section 9 that said that *nothing in this Act shall permit the Crown to act in a manner that is inconsistent with the principles of the Treaty of Waitangi* – I think that's what we said.

People have complained that the Act was a rushed job. How did Sir Geoffrey see it?

> I think we did that Act in about three or four weeks, from memory. We had quite a small team working on it and they were very good. And it took a bit longer to get it through, but the actual design of it, I doubt whether it took more than a couple of months anyway.

Dr Brash claims in the Orewa speech that section 9 was poorly drafted and thrown in at the last minute. Sir Geoffrey agrees that it went in at the last minute.

> But it wasn't poorly drafted and there's nothing wrong with its drafting. The difficulty that he raises, though, is a different one. It is that one should not put Treaty clauses in legislation because they don't have an ascertainable content. That's a different point and that's quite a good point . . . It'd be better to figure out what

> you mean to do rather than use these generalised formulae, and in retrospect I agree with that.

Some context: the Act came into force at the end of 1986, and the lands were due to be handed over to the SOEs in May 1987. Maori looked at the Act and didn't like what they found. It seemed to them that a lot of land might be at risk that wasn't covered by section 27. What about tribes that hadn't laid a claim before the transfer had occurred? What about tribes that might not know that they had a right to claim lands that had been taken under the Public Works Act 1981 and wouldn't now be used for that purpose?

They took an injunction against the transfer of Crown land that duly found them in the Court of Appeal, arguing before five judges on a case that would have far-reaching effects.

The Court found that, thanks to section 9 of the SOE Act, the Treaty of Waitangi prevented the Crown from transferring land to SOEs without entering into proper arrangements to protect Maori claims.

Sir Geoffrey says he didn't think section 9 was going to carry the weight that the Court of Appeal subsequently gave it.

> They read that up and they read section 27 down and I was a bit surprised at that. And the Cabinet wanted us to appeal that and I said, 'We're not taking this to London. This is absolutely not an appropriate subject to go to London.' And so we effectively settled that case by another piece of legislation in 1988 which allowed the Tribunal to actually make settlements out of SOE land.

Problem solved? Well, yes, that particular problem. But in hindsight we can see that the words of those judges of the Court of Appeal would have some far-reaching consequences. Firstly, there was the way they interpreted the principles of the Treaty of Waitangi, and secondly there was one specific word they used that would come to mean a very great deal: 'partnership'. It wasn't long before some broad, vaguely defined ideas were working their way into the bureaucracy, and once that happened, things began to get *really* interesting.

CHAPTER EIGHT: PARTNERS IN TIME

'They talk about these principles, but no one knows what they are'

> 'The Treaty signified a partnership between races, and it is in this concept that the answer to the present case has to be found . . .'
>
> ROBIN COOKE, NZ MAORI COUNCIL V. ATTORNEY-GENERAL

ONE OF my favourite cartoons is of a large elephant surrounded by men with white canes and dark glasses. Each of them is using his hands to help describe what they can't see. One of them is holding its trunk and declaring: *An elephant is like a snake*. One has climbed on its back: *An elephant is like a brush*. One is holding his leg: *An elephant is like a tree trunk*. One of them is holding its tail: *An elephant is like a rope*. A few paces behind the elephant, the other blind man is investigating a small pile of something that would, a few moments earlier, have exited the elephant. *An elephant is soft and mushy*, he announces.

Definitions can be tricky things, especially when you don't have the full picture to work from: 147 years after the event, the Court of Appeal set out to define what it was the parties to the

Treaty had signed at Waitangi, and as we've seen, they delivered a very significant judgment. A lot of people were beginning to ask: *What does the Treaty of Waitangi mean?*

It was mentioned in statutes now – which meant that people who had to follow the laws of those statutes needed to know what it meant. Secondly, because it now appeared in statute the courts were actually able to have regard to it, so they would be asking the question. As well as that, it was starting to appear more often in the news, as the claims began to stack up. The public, Parliament, the bureaucrats all wanted to know what it said, exactly. And they were finding that it wasn't entirely clear.

So when the Court of Appeal came riding in with a considered assessment of the thing, people got quite excited. As we've seen, the Court held that the Crown couldn't transfer land to SOEs without entering into proper arrangements to protect Maori claims, and the Government duly made changes to the legislation to put that right. But the far-reaching influence of the case would be the reasoning the Justices used to come to the decisions. It offered some guidance on how to interpret the meaning of the Treaty in any given situation, and it tried to answer the question: What *are* the principles of the Treaty of Waitangi that the State-Owned Enterprises Act refers to? Amongst other things, the Court found that:

> The Treaty signified a partnership between Pakeha and Maori requiring each to act towards the other reasonably and with the utmost good faith. The relationship between the Treaty partners creates responsibilities analogous to fiduciary duties. The duty of the Crown is not merely passive but extends to active protection of Maori people in the use of their lands and waters to the fullest extent practicable. That duty is no light one and is infinitely more than a formality. If a breach of the duty is demonstrated at any time, the duty of the Court will be to insist that it be honoured.

> It will be seen that approaching the case independently we have all reached two major conclusions. First that the principles of the Treaty of Waitangi override everything else in the State-Owned Enterprises Act. Second that those principles require the Pakeha and Maori Treaty partners to act towards each other reasonably and with the utmost good faith.
>
> From the attitude of the Colonial Office and the transactions between its representatives and the Maori chiefs, and from the terms of the Treaty itself, it is not difficult to infer the start in 1840 of something in the nature of a partnership between the Crown and the Maori people.

The word in the judgments that took on the most significance for many was *partnership*. But the first thing that might strike you is that it seems to be used to illustrate a point, rather than something more emphatic. The court might well have agreed with you, but that didn't stop a lot of people from grabbing the word and bolting it onto their Treaty of Waitangi policies. Alex Frame:

> I confess that I'm wary of this expression 'partnership'. I don't think it gets you to the fundamentals. Partnership, in my view, is an outcome. And it's an outcome of what? It's an outcome of co-operation. Co-operation is the more fundamental concept.
>
> But let me say that co-operation – it sounds easy doesn't it, but it's quite a sophisticated concept, and [there are] a number of features of co-operation. Let's just think about some of them.
>
> For you and I to think about moving this couch into another room, what do we have to do? Well, we have to have an understanding of what we're trying to do. We needn't necessarily be doing the same things, you might be stronger, but I might be able to sort of manoeuvre through the door better because I'm smaller – so the contributions don't have to be symmetrical.
>
> There has to be solicitude for one another. It's not going to work if you break your back, or if I bark my knuckles – we have to look after each other.
>
> So that, it seems to me, co-operation is the fundamental

concept. Now, if you co-operate together, if people see us with this couch, manoeuvring it around and getting it in, they might well say, 'Oh, these people seem to have some sort of partnership going.' They might say that.

But my criticism of the partnership concept is therefore twofold: one, it doesn't get to the root of the matter, and it diverts you off into less fruitful second-level stuff about, 'Oh well, there's meant to be a partnership, should be an equal number on each side of the table, how many positions . . .'

My second objection flows from that and it is that it's not operationally useful. If you're trying to operationalise, you're needing to give guidance to second- and third-level management – at the desk level, at the counter level. To say to that person, 'Oh, you should be in partnership with iwi,' I think confronts people with something that's basically unhelpful. So what does that mean?

Whereas if the guidance is that we should be co-operating, properly understood, in my view, that's a concept which is generally understood by people. People know, and they can instantly recognise when there's not co-operation – through body language alone.

So, co-operation. And I said in writing that I thought that, with the greatest respect, the Court of Appeal, if you like, embedded that partnership concept in the 1987 *Lands* decision. [They] might have developed their thinking a bit further, and had they done so, I believe, had they dug deeper, they might have come to the realisation that there is a more fundamental category involved. So, if you like, in philosophers' language, it's a category mistake.

This is where it gets interesting. The bureaucracies get hold of the word *partnership*, some of the folks in the bureaucracy get a bit excited about the idea of a *partnership*, and start talking about *our partner*, and doing some rather improbable things in the name of showing appropriate recognition to the *partner*.

Did the Treaty train start running off the track? Suppose a statute that affects your ministry tells you to act in a manner consistent with the Treaty of Waitangi, but leaves it up to you to decide what that means. You look around, and everyone seems to be using this *partnership* word. Nothing spreads around Wellington like a *mot-du-jour*. And suddenly you get some eager and awfully well-intentioned people looking for ways in which to work together as *partners* – an obligation to consult in scientific research, for example. Could this have arisen out of that kind of interpretation going awry? Frame again:

> Yes. That's the kind of error – what I call the category mistake – precisely the kind of error that it's likely to lead you into, creating a sense of expectation that there's some kind of mechanical process, a 50/50 process ... I think that the rather mechanical concept of partnership has led us up some false pathways.

Sir Douglas Graham agrees. But he points out that the judgment wasn't quite as emphatic as people seem to have taken it to be.

> Bear in mind that only Robin Cooke said that. He was the one who said it. He thought this was 'a partnership'. The other judges ... said it was *like* a partnership. The obligations I have are like the obligations you have in a partnership – good faith, openness, frankness – and I don't have any problem about that. I've spoken with Duncan McMullin often enough since – and the other judges who sat on the case – who said, 'We never intended it to be some sort of joint government. That was never the intention.'
>
> He was as flabbergasted as anybody. But once it got legs in the bureaucracy ... I used to sit in the cabinet committees when the officials were there and I said, 'Look, all this business about partnership, why are you putting this in? We can have an open debate, we can help and assist, do all those things, act honestly, but the government's sovereign, that's the end of it.' The Treaty actually says that it's a government for everybody. But this concept of partnership ... it was a very unfortunate word.

The court itself had more to say about this in a later judgment, where it pointed out that partnership did *not* mean a 50/50 deal and shouldn't be interpreted that way.

So, if we've decided one thing we *shouldn't* interpret the Treaty to mean, it still leaves us wondering what it *does* mean. This is where a handy Government booklet comes in, the *Principles for Crown Action on the Treaty of Waitangi*, produced in 1989 with the aim of clarifying the Crown's approach to Treaty issues and to give guidance to government agencies on how these issues should be handled. I know a little about this because I was working in the Beehive at the time, and carried it around in my briefcase for a while with Secret stamped on it in large, forbidding letters.

The irony of it is that some people still seem to think it's secret, given the way they complain about the 'principles' of the Treaty being unknowable. There have been other attempts to define this contested territory, but this document does a very good job of contemplating the fairest outcome for all parties. It distils the thinking of all the bodies that had already been considering the Treaty – the Courts, the Waitangi Tribunal, the Law Commission, the New Zealand Maori Council. Here are the five principles it identified:

The Principle of Government – The Kawanatanga Principle

This confirms that Maori handed over sovereignty to the Crown under the Treaty, and that gives it the right to make laws and run a government. However, there's a very important qualification to that, and that is that under Article II it has to give Maori interests an appropriate priority.

This statement from the Waitangi Tribunal in the Te Atiawa report is offered as an example of what is meant:

> That then was the exchange of gifts that the Treaty represented. The gift of the right to make laws and the promise to do so, so as to accord the Maori interest an appropriate priority.

It is pointed out that it's not unusual for New Zealand to submit to some limitation on what it can do as a sovereign nation. It routinely enters into international treaties in which it undertakes to be bound by international commitments in trade, human rights, transportation and so on.

The Principle of Self-Management – The Rangatiratanga Principle

This recognises that iwi Maori have the right to control and enjoy the resources and taonga they want to keep. The Government has to do what it can to help them keep their resource base, restore iwi self-management and protect their taonga – their treasures – both material and cultural. The statement says this is crucial, because without it Maori wouldn't have signed away their sovereignty.

It points out that the Court of Appeal said:

> The duty of the Crown is not merely passive but extends to active protection of Maori people in the use of their lands and waters to the fullest extent practicable.

Also noted is that the Waitangi Tribunal had made clear that the expression 'taonga' extended also to language and other cultural treasures. In clarifying the interpretation of the Treaty, the Tribunal had looked at the instructions Lord Normanby gave to Captain Hobson; specifically, not to permit the acquisition of lands to a degree which would cause 'distress or serious inconvenience to Maori'. Therefore, the Tribunal concluded, if you were going to achieve that promise to protect rangatiratanga, you had to ensure that iwi kept a basic endowment of land and resources.

But what did 'rangatiratanga' mean, exactly? The Waitangi Tribunal had found that:

> The Maori text thus conveyed an intention that the Maori would retain full authority over their lands, homes and things important to them or, in a phrase, they would retain their Mana Maori . . .
>
> (Orakei Report, 1987, p. 134)

And the New Zealand Maori Council had explained the concept as meaning more than 'possession':

> It means the wise administration of all the assets possessed by a group for that group's benefit: in a word: trusteeship.
>
> (Te Wahanga Tuatahi, 1983, p. 5)

The upshot was this:

> The First and Second Articles of the Treaty are both strong statements which necessarily qualify one another. Kawanatanga is subject to a promise to protect rangatiratanga. Rangatiratanga is subject to an acknowledgment of kawanatanga. The working out in practice of the balance between the two articles must depend on a case by case consideration. Clearly 'tino rangatiratanga' (or 'full chieftainship') will generally take precedence in matters concerning material and cultural resources and taonga which have been retained. Equally, however, where there can be clearly demonstrated a danger to all, or a general need which can be managed only at the level of national action, the Crown must exercise its power on behalf of all New Zealand citizens. To take but one simple example, the control of dangerous substances (such as radioactive material, poisons etc.) could only be effective under a legislative regime which speaks for all citizens and to all situations. It is the *right* of all citizens, Maori, Pakeha and other New Zealanders, that there be effective Government or kawanatanga in such matters.

Notice those words – *case by case*. If you want to work out what it means, look at the specific issue in front of you, any other way will tie you up in knots. This from the *Lands* case is given to support the idea:

> The principles of the Treaty do not authorise unreasonable restrictions on the right of a duly elected government to follow its chosen policy. Indeed to try and shackle the Government unreasonably would itself be inconsistent with those principles. The test of reasonableness is necessarily a broad one and necessarily has to be applied by the Court in the end in a realistic way. The parties owe each other co-operation.

The message was clear: you have to balance the two against each other, and you have to do it in an intelligent way. As the Law Commission had said:

> The Treaty gave the Crown what it sought: sovereignty and governance over New Zealand. This is a continuing authority and power. What the Maori received in return is likewise ongoing – the continued protection of the rights that the Treaty acknowledged as theirs …

The Principle of Equality

This said that the third article of the Treaty made all New Zealand citizens equal before the law. It said that it saw the 'rights and privileges of British subjects' as something that changes over time. The Court of Appeal had held that the Treaty was a living document, which means you can read it that way. So what are everyone's rights today? Not just what you get under the heritage of a legal tradition going back to Magna Carta, but also the rights which New Zealand has promised its citizens in modern times, including its rights under international conventions.

If you liked what Don Brash had to say about 'special treatment and benefits for Maori', see what you think of this: the definition of 'rangatiratanga' also argued that if there is a serious and persistent imbalance between groups, in their actual enjoyment of social benefits such as health, education or housing, then government will consider particular measures to assist in redressing the balance. Article 1(4) of the International Convention on the Elimination of All Forms of Racial Discrimination of 1966, which came into force for New Zealand in 1972, expressly recognises that such special measures 'shall not be deemed racial discrimination' provided they are not continued after imbalance is remedied.

The Principle of Co-operation

This argued that responsible co-operation can only take place if there is consultation on major issues of common concern and if good faith, balance and common sense are shown on all sides.

It referred to other elements that the Courts and the Waitangi Tribunal had identified: good faith, consultation and partnership, and it made a very interesting point:

> It is co-operation which signals the difference between the distinctive cultural development guaranteed by the Treaty (if desired on the Maori side) and that 'apartheid' which has rightly attracted the condemnation of the modern world.

It also quotes the Royal Commission on Social Policy in its report in 1988:

> The Treaty of Waitangi was not about sameness or the introduction of one social order at the expense of the other. By providing for diversity within agreed understandings, a basis was established for co-operation, and participation between old and new.

The Principle of Redress

It points out here that redress is desirable even though the Treaty doesn't mention it, and it quotes the *Lands* case:

> ... where grievances are established, the State for its part is required to take positive steps in reparation.

And how should the Government go about it? It says that it should have regard to the practical impact of a measure. You should look at the economic and administrative feasibility, the need to spread the cost and the benefits, and bear in mind that it be acceptable to, or at least tolerated by a reasonably broad range of opinion. In saying that, it recalls the Waitangi Tribunal's warning that:

> It is out of keeping with the spirit of the Treaty that the resolution of one injustice should be seen to create another.

By the end of the 1980s, a good body of careful analysis had built up that told us what the Treaty 'principles' might be. The question now was how well those principles might be applied.

TEST YOUR TREATY KNOWLEDGE 7

Who has the final say in a Treaty settlement?

A. The Waitangi Tribunal
B. The Court of Appeal
C. The Privy Council
D. Parliament
E. Winston Peters

(Answers page 199)

CHAPTER NINE: EARLY SETTLEMENT

'It's easy to make a settlement when you're writing cheques with someone else's money.'

A FRIEND told me this story: he was involved with Ngai Tahu for a time, and he would go to speak at meetings around Christchurch – Rotary, business groups, that kind of thing – about the Ngai Tahu claim:

> I'd go in there and they'd all have their arms folded across their chests, you know – *What's all this bullshit?* – and yet, by the end they'd be angry. Not at what I'd had to say, but at what they'd found out. And they'd say, *Why didn't we know about this?* They had no idea what had been done to these people, and they had no idea how Maori had been cheated, lied to and swindled.

Well, at the Waitangi Tribunal it all came out. To give you an idea of the kind of evidence they heard, take a look first at the Ngati Whatua claim, which came right at the beginning of the new regime allowing for historical investigations.

In 1840, Apihai Te Kawau, the paramount chief of Ngati Whatua invited Governor Hobson to make Auckland the seat of government, and he offered him 3000 acres for the purpose

– the land that would become Parnell, the CBD, Ponsonby, Grey Lynn, Herne Bay and some of Newmarket and Mt Eden.

In 1841 a gathering of 1000 Ngati Whatua greeted Hobson on the shores of Okahu Bay. Te Kawau addressed him: 'Governor, Governor, welcome as a father to me. There is land for you ... go and pick the best part of the land and place your people, at least our people upon it.' He chose the land that is today Westmere, Pt Chevalier, Western Springs, Waterview, Avondale, Mt Albert, Titirangi, Sandringham, Mt Roskill, Three Kings, Balmoral, Kingsland, Mt Eden and Epsom – another 8000 acres.

Te Kawau made the gesture because he could see the potential of an alliance – in exchange, they could expect commerce, education and health, and the protection of all under the law. Instead, what they got was endless pressure to sell more land. Within five years, Ngati Whatua had seen over 100,000 acres disappear with little to show for it. By 1868 they were reduced to the 700-acre Orakei Block. The Native Land Court put a classification on it: 'forever inalienable', never to be sold. Forever ran out just before the First World War. While Ngati Whatua leaders were overseas with New Zealand troops, the Government passed a law allowing for the individualisation of title. It was the old divide-and-rule approach – make it possible for just a few of the owners to sign away the rights, and everyone else loses out. The land was sold off and what remained was a marae, a pa and an urupa based at Okahu Bay.

In 1951 the Auckland City Council decided that the marae and pa were an eyesore on Tamaki Drive and unsafe for habitation. They evicted all residents and put them in new state housing on the Kupe St hill. And then they knocked over and burned the marae and the buildings around it to the ground. The quarter-acre cemetery was all that was left – the last piece of land they could tribally claim as their own.

So when the Government planned to subdivide the land on Bastion Point, why wouldn't Ngati Whatua object? It was their land, and it still would have been, if the Crown had done what it was supposed to under the Treaty. It should have vested the land that was left in 1854 – the 700-acre Orakei Block – in Ngati Whatua. It should have stopped the Native Land Court from circumventing the requirement that all customary owners should be named in a title. It should have helped the tribe retain the marae site and the farmlands. There was more, but you get the picture. The Tribunal agreed with them. It said the Crown had failed in its duty under the Treaty. It should have ensured that Maori were left with enough land for their economic and social wellbeing.

The tenor of the Tribunal's approach to interpreting the Treaty was also clear – you didn't look at the words finely, you looked at the broad context: *Why did the parties go into the Treaty? What did they expect to come out of it?* It looked back to the wider historical context and at Normanby's instructions to Hobson, for example. It assessed the intentions of the Crown, and the understanding of the Maori chiefs.

It's hard to argue with this: giving effect to what people intended is surely the best basis for sorting things out when the document itself is not clear. This is where some of the more foam-flecked writers about the so-called 'Treaty Scandal' seem to part company with those supposedly 'in on' the scandal. *Look at the spelling in this line here*, they say. *Look at this missing draft that was discovered under my great-aunt's hatbox. These four words here make it clear that Maori knew what they were doing and they gave away everything*. The Tribunal has typically taken the view that more sense can be made of it only if the Treaty's overall aim and purpose is considered.

The Tribunal's approach at this point was largely in line with the Government's own *Principles for Crown Action* (echoing what academics and historians had been bringing to light for some years). The two bodies would later drift apart in their interpretation of other aspects of claims, but for now they were pretty much in step.

And so the Government readily adopted the Tribunal's recommendations. It handed back 67 hectares of public reserves and parks to Ngati Whatua. The public would still have access, and control of the land would be vested in a reserves board comprising Ngati Whatua and Auckland City Council representatives. The Orakei Marae land was also vested in Ngati Whatua. The Ngati Whatua board was given an extra 3 hectares of land for future development and $3 million for programmes that might help the rehabilitation of the tribe.

It was a pretty good example of a settlement that restored mana without taking any land from anyone or causing great expense to the taxpayer. Considering how much had been lost, it was little enough, but it resolved the grievance.

It was clear the Tribunal was willing to recognise historical grievances and recommend action. The way it was interpreting the Treaty and its principles made it clear – it would be looking to the spirit of the Treaty and the context in which it was signed. It would be recognising that the way Maori owned their land was different: it was tribal and communal – it should have been protected as a community resource and as the basis of tribal cohesion. Where there was a Treaty obligation and it had been broken, Maori would be entitled to compensation.

Not everyone thought this was good news.

If you were reading the papers or watching the TV news back then, you might recall the *sky-is-falling* mood of the times. The papers said, *This'll cost a fortune.* The politicians said, *This'll cost a fortune. Untold millions. People will have their homes taken from them.*

Actually it's worth pausing to look at this, because it scares people. The only possibility that the Tribunal can ever order the return of land is in the case of land that's been transferred under the SOE Act. That's what the *Lands* case was about. And land that's been transferred in that way can be ordered by the Tribunal to be compulsorily acquired, for compensation from whoever owns it, and returned. That also applies to coal, commercial forest land and the value of its tree crop, and tertiary institute land. The fact that it has this liability gets written on the title – should you ever come to buy such a piece of land. On top of that, there's even another act passed in 1993 which expressly says that the Tribunal can't recommend that any private land be returned to Maori ownership or acquired by the Crown.

So there was a lot of fretting going on – maps in the newspapers showing how much of the country *those Maoris* wanted to have handed over to them. More than a decade down the road, we know that it didn't turn out that way, of course, but that didn't stop the politicians from giving the whole thing a good working over. Winston Peters had plenty to say; so did Jim Bolger. There's always an election coming up. And if you're in opposition, one of the best things you can do is scare people about things that *might* happen. Better yet, point to things that *are* happening, extrapolate it out and plot a scary trajectory. There was plenty of that. But Jim Bolger came to see the justice of it, and he would end up playing no small part in dealing effectively with some of the biggest claims.

What was clear from the early Tribunal decisions and the throng of claimants quickly joining a queue was that the Government would have to start working out what to do about the claims they were going to have to settle.

The Tribunal would be hearing claims on many things: wrongful confiscation of lands; promised payment, or reserves of land that were never delivered; appropriation of natural resources, such as water rights, geothermal rights, fishing rights being used without agreement or payment; non-return of gifted land, such as land gifted for a school which was not returned when it became surplus to requirements; insufficient recognition of sacred sites; land acquired for one purpose but used for another; the loss of cultural treasures, such as the past discouragement of the use of the Maori language; non-recognition of rights based on Article III of the Treaty in relation to the equal treatment of Maori and non-Maori. There would be a settling-up for all of this, and someone would have to pay.

Alex Frame was involved in the Government's first tentative steps towards working out a process for settling grievances.

> I think the most important thing that happened at that time was that Government decided to break away from the earlier full and final settlements. In 1944 and '46, settlements had been reached in respect of Tainui claims for confiscated lands – raupatu – and also Ngai Tahu in the South Island. They were described as full and final in much clearer language than any of the modern settlements, so that was clearly a real problem for Government: what to do about those settlements in the face of claims much more broadly based, much more extensive claims.
>
> Tainui, I think, ended up with a final offer something in the nature of $20 million. People say, 'Oh, look, they ended up getting 170, you were pretty mean.' But I sometimes say it was probably as hard to get from nought to twenty as it was to get from twenty to 170, and the reason is simply that there were, on the books, statutes saying unequivocally that these were full and final settlements, as well as a good deal of historical material indicating that this was the case. For example, there's a famous telegram from Te Puea to Fraser, I think, saying, 'Okay,

this is the end of the matter, thank you very much. Everything is done.'

What had they settled on?

I remember seeing somewhere where it was asked how Fraser reached the figure of, I think it was something like 5000 pounds per year as a perpetual annuity ... I think the answer was something like: well, at a rough guess, it was the ability to buy one farm each year in perpetuity.

With the contemplation that in the very long term you might get back to the acreage that was confiscated?

I suppose so. One of the things that upset that calculation, and I think in the end made it inevitable that Government would revisit it ... was [that it was] not indexed in some way. Because, of course, by the 1970s–1980s, 5000 pounds – $10,000 – was a risible sum. You simply couldn't buy a farm for that, which [you] might have done in 1945 and '46.

So it was accepted that unforeseen circumstances had arisen that extinguished the effectiveness of earlier settlements?

Yes it did. We commissioned studies to see:, What if settlements had kept pace with inflation? Where would we be? ... Obviously a much greater figure.

From the point of view of the Labour Government of the day, I think that Fraser and his advisers thought that it was really just a matter of ... land and farms, but that this wasn't, essentially, a political claim. I think that what they'd failed to realise and what had become apparent by the 1980s was that it wasn't simply about acres and dollars, but that also lying behind the whole Maori claim was an aspiration for Mana Motuhake, the preservation of Maori mana, language, culture – and in fact the Maori feel in New Zealand, that New Zealand should feel like – partly at least – a Maori place.

It must have been about 1989 – and don't forget this was before Doug Graham came onto the scene – I was instructed

> by Cabinet to lead the negotiations. We took a team to Dame Te Atairangikaahu's house in Waikato, and there was a lockup there ... with Bob Mahuta and his team. And I remember one session, there were two Tainui kuia there, and I remember one of them breaking down at one point and saying that they felt like orphans. That was the word she used. And that made an impression on me, and I think if you look at the ultimate apology, I think you'll find that word is there, it was certainly there in a draft that I did of it and I promised her – that kuia – that I would see that sentiment was explained there.
>
> So that took us through to the change of government ... and the minister of the day, Bill Jeffries, made an offer just before the 1990 election, which Tainui turned down. As I say, it equated to about $20 million in terms of land returned and cash and so on.
>
> And Doug Graham then came on the scene, and I think it's a tribute to his vision and his ability to empathise that he got things moving again pretty quickly and pretty decisively, established a rapport with Sir Bob Mahuta and then the negotiations became much more complicated and much more extensive ... As you know, history tells us that that went on to the approximately $170 million settlement.

Matthew Palmer was Crown Negotiator for Treasury during the first historical settlement with Waikato Tainui. He now thinks the settlement process has become too mechanistic, whereas it had originally just evolved in the doing.

> We knew we wanted a deal. We knew there were some things the Government couldn't live with and there were some things it could live with, and the same was true of Tainui. The thing was to work out what would satisfy both parties to the extent that they believed that this would settle the grievance, and I think that was satisfied there.
>
> What then happened was that – as government officials tend to do – you can then analyse that deal and say ... we're going to construct a new process and a new menu of options and just apply that to everyone else.

> Ngai Tahu took it a step further – I mean you're talking about significant non-financial redress in terms of access to various different places and conservation estate which was off the table in the Tainui deal. So there was an evolution, but after those two settlements you started to get a bit of a template approach. You'd have a much smaller grievance come up and officials would say, 'Ah, we know how to do this …'
>
> To the extent that that works, that's fine. But to the extent that it doesn't work, you've actually got to take a step back as the Crown and say, 'What do you actually want to get?' And again, that will have to be on a very individual basis of that iwi – and the question of who you negotiate with is another complication.

Complex though those two big settlements were, they were simple by comparison with later ones such as Taranaki and the Muriwhenua negotiations, where different groups with their own agendas and objectives made bargaining such a tortuous process. Says Palmer, it's understandable that the Government would want to simplify things as much as possible.

> They're basically trying to get these done as soon as they can. It's much easier for a big bureaucratic system to work with a known set of quantities, to work with mechanisms and tools it understands. But I think you need to bear in mind what the ultimate objective is – which is to settle a grievance in the minds of the people you're settling with. Because otherwise there's no point.

TEST YOUR TREATY KNOWLEDGE 8

Tertiary students have access to 1451 scholarships for study. How many more scholarships are available solely to Maori?

- A. 154
- B. 238
- C. 487
- D. 968
- E. 2489

(Answers page 199)

CHAPTER TEN: MONEY JUSTICE

'That's the last we'll see of that money. How much more will they want?'

THE GREAT thing about the Treaty settlements, you may recall, is that everyone quickly came to see that it was the right thing to do, and urged the Government to hand over as much money as possible as soon as it could. This all happened in early 1996, a couple of weeks after hell froze over.

Ask around and you'll still find people who think the whole thing is a travesty. And even if you can persuade them that there have been injustices, they still have their 'yes, but' answers ready. They tell you that the money's not going into the right pockets, and that they'll be back again for more. Sir Douglas Graham sees it this way:

> I think if we were able to settle each of the land claims and get each of the tribes some cash, economic clout, then they get political clout, then they've got something to offer the Maori people – a new focus, [it] lifts them up in esteem, and all of a sudden the risk of being swamped and assimilated is gone; Ngai Tahu are going around recording all the old people's stories – it's great – and scholarships for kids and ... the idea that you

should have divided up the settlement money and given them $10 each – Act was on about this – is just madness. These tribal members today didn't lose a thing: the *tribe* lost. So the tribe is the one that gets recompense. What the tribe decides to do with it is entirely a matter for them. Now [some people are] saying that they'll blow the lot and come back again. *I don't think so.*

Can a full and final settlement have lasting effect? Matthew Palmer believes the historical settlements are important, because you can't actually make progress otherwise.

... If you look at Ngai Tahu for example – Tainui's another example, but in a different way. But Ngai Tahu, the relationships are going ahead in a way which they weren't before the settlements.

Was that because it was a more all-embracing settlement than had been achieved at the end of the Second World War?

Yes. It was actually something that meant something to them – they had negotiated it. They said what they wanted, they got some of that. So these policies which people come up with that say, 'We're going to have a policy to just settle all the grievances by a certain date' – it's artificial because there's only any point in settling a grievance if the people who are aggrieved believe it's settled. They're not going to believe it's settled if you impose some arbitrary time frame on it. They've got to believe it's settled, otherwise why bother?

Of course, there are aspects to the process that make you wonder a little. Tom Bennion points out that there is no cut-off as such in the current claims process.

If a person comes to [your] office and says *Can I lodge another claim?* you say *Well, yes.* The only thing that rules it out at the moment is if they've got a claim settlement that pretty much covers the bases, so that there's really nothing you can do – it's in statute. There are clauses that say there are to be no further claims – you might try to argue around those clauses, but those clauses are one cut-off.

Even if someone argued around them if the settlement's in place, though … take the Ngai Tahu claim, what are you going to say? They've got a big argument – they think there's a big hole in the middle of the South Island that the Tribunal concluded they have sold. And I think there's a pretty good argument that that's probably a weak conclusion of the Tribunal. But so what? I mean … they're getting on with business. If they're still running things this way in ten years', fifteen years' time, no one's really going to have anything to complain about.

But should there be cut-offs? This is the other thing that comes up – should there be close-off dates for claims? People just don't appreciate how much the Tribunal is thinking about that. Some hapu are now being heard in as little as half a day. I've represented a group that had its whole claim heard in about five hours. That's how tight the process is. And I've been to meetings where the Tribunal's said, 'How can we speed it up further? – we've got to go faster than this …'

The Tribunal is going hell for leather … you've got keen Maori leaders in there saying, 'We're not waiting another fifteen years because, on current rates, we can't have iwi ten years down the track that haven't got a settlement.' That's unjust now. That's got to be unjust … The Tribunal, before it goes and sits in a district, issues a public notice. The public notice says 'Get your claims in right now because if you don't, sure, we can't say we won't hear them, but you're going to wait a long time.'

Another argument thrown in the face of the Treaty process is this: that *there are no real full-blooded Maori any more,* that the whole issue of ethnic identification has become arbitrary. Has it? We may not know who an individual Maori is, but we do know there are Maori here. And it's fairly clear that they've got some sort of cultural identity, and it's fairly clear they want to assert it. Some people claim we're all becoming one big mixture of New Zealanders – but really that's what the Hunn Report was aiming for, assimilating Maori and turning them into brown

Pakeha. As we've seen, Maori identity actually developed and strengthened in the decades that followed.

Sir Tipene O'Regan points out that Maori have never been so demographically concentrated as they are now.

> ... There are more and more, they are younger and younger, and they are urban. That hasn't stopped the bulk of them from identifying through their iwi.
>
> Now, the other thing that drives the society's politics and discourse is the fact that there's just so many more. In 1840 – or even if we go pre-musket – there were probably no more than about three to four thousand Ngai Tahu, and that would be stretching it. Today there are just under 40,000.
>
> ... There's something like 28,000 on the Ngai Tahu register – that is, they've actually had to go through the process and register, make statutory declarations and make whakapapa connections and all that sort of thing, out of the total group of 40,000 who identify for census purposes.

That raises an important point. Settlements are being made with iwi rather than individuals, and the benefits get allocated by iwi, rather than individuals. (Not in the case of fisheries, but we'll get to that in a minute.) That puts plenty on the iwi register and helps you when you have to allocate the benefits of a settlement. Margaret Wilson explains that reparations ...

> ... were made to basically settle the grievances on the basis, not of a people – the Maori people – but of being specific to events that related to particular hapu or iwi. And that was a recognition of the essence of Maori society as tribal.
>
> Now, there are some who would argue that by recognising that you're embedding and instilling the tribalism, and that's not conducive to people going forward. That is another debate and argument. But for better or worse, it's done. And that's the dilemma, to some extent, that some urban Maori have – how do those people benefit from a settlement process that is based on a tribal membership?

So you leave it to iwi to work out how to share it around wisely?

> Absolutely and it won't matter whether you're living in an urban centre or in a rural setting. But it will require good management and accountabilities and internal organisation with those iwis.

John Tamihere sees it differently. Where do urban Maori fit into all of this?

> ... They're the bridge. Always have been and always will be. And if we took a proper legal approach to Treaty settlements, they'd be restitutional. And there are Privy Council decisions on it that the restitution follows the beneficiaries. It doesn't follow a reconstructed corporate office in Paeroa or Ruatoria where none of us live – what that lends itself to is the rise of a feudal elite, and actually we *were* a meritocracy. Primogeniture was just one measure of the pecking order. So if you didn't live up to it, your line jumped.
>
> So we've got a huge disconnection between the people forming assets and the people forming communities – and how crazy is that?

It's worth bearing in mind, however, that settlements aren't intended to take care of all the problems that Maori face. They're supposed to remedy some particular Treaty breaches that harmed particular iwi. You still need social policy to deal with other problems Maori face, as we'll see in a moment.

What about the process itself, though? How much longer is it going to drag on? Margaret Wilson:

> We're trying to go for three deeds a year, and if we can get three acts accordingly, that'd be good. And if we do the large natural groupings negotiations, then ten to fifteen years is not unrealistic in terms of settling the majority of the claims.

Just how much money are we talking about? According to the Office of Treaty Settlements, the total cost of settlements since

1989 has been $596 million. Sound like a lot of money? Well, maybe. But let's put it into perspective. The Government collected $57 billion in total for the year ending June 2003 – so in the simplest terms, if you're worrying about all this money sending the country broke, you can stop fretting. In terms of the amounts the Government deals with, it's slight. Very slight. According to Treasury, in the past five years, the Government has spent $227 billion. Treaty settlements in that period totalled $248 million, or 0.109 per cent of total spending.

That means that if you paid $1,000,000 in tax in the last five years, your contribution to Treaty settlements was $1090. If you paid $100,000 in tax in the last five years, your contribution to treaty settlements was $109.

Now take a look down the street where you live and total up the value of the houses. Then multiply it by ten or twenty streets. Starts to add up pretty fast, doesn't it? My apologies if you live in the country. Try the same calculation by totting up the value of the nearest dozen farms and multiply that by ten or twenty. Now compare that to, say, all the land in the Waikato, or Taranaki, or the South Island. How's that $600 million looking now?

This isn't just a question of money, but to the extent that people have this idea that the settlements and the *Treaty Industry* are costing a fortune, it's equally arguable that this is a pretty small price to pay for restoring justice, for transferring back some of the enormous economic power Maori held when the new nation was getting under way. If it helps to get more Maori into better, more productive, more purposeful lives, isn't it worth it?

Of course, you might say that this is just the tip of the iceberg, that there's a colossal mountain of claims still to go. Well, not really. Let's look at the numbers. According to the Office of

Treaty Settlements, there have been fifteen completed settlements since 1989:

Ngati Tama
$14.5 million

Ngati Ruanui
$41 million

Te Uri o Hau
$15.6 million

Pouakani
$2.65 million

Ngati Turangitukua
$5 million

Ngai Tahu
$170 million

Te Maunga
$129,032

Rotoma
$43,931

Waimakuku
$375,000

Waikato/Tainui raupatu
$170 million

Ngati Whakaue
$5.21 million

Haui
$715,682

Commercial Fisheries
$170 million

Ngati Rangiteaorere
$760,000

Waitomo
The Crown transferred land at the Waitomo Caves to the claimant group, subject to a lease, and provided a loan of $1 million.

You may have heard or read about claims numbering in the hundreds or even thousands. But that's because you start out with a great many that then get consolidated into one large one, taking all the separate claims by individuals from the same tribal group. That's why Margaret Wilson is forecasting three deeds a year, taking ten to fifteen years to square it all away.

And then there's the long and complicated business of fish. The story of the fisheries is really one of the Government professing to do one thing, and effectively doing the opposite. Over the 150 years following the Treaty, it passed various acts protecting Maori fishing rights, but in practice, it eroded them.

It all came to a head in the 1980s when the Ministry of Agriculture and Fisheries set up a Quota Management System for fisheries. Nice idea – the resource was being depleted by overfishing, so you ration it and make quotas a tradeable commodity. The bad news was that it didn't recognise that Maori fishing rights existed. Those rights were protected by the Treaty, and if you were going to turn fishing rights into a property you could buy and sell, then you would first have to compensate Maori for it, in the view of a number of tribes who had already lodged land and fisheries claims with the Tribunal.

Let's think back a moment: the Treaty says in words that couldn't be clearer that their fisheries are protected. It recognises their ownership. Did Maori give up that right? Don't think so. You might think the smart thing would have been to wait and see what the Tribunal had to say, and work out what to do about that, but the Ministry pressed ahead anyway. In the end, though, the Tribunal told them that what Maori had claimed was true. They said the tribes of Muriwhenua had established conclusively that their fishing had been very extensive, highly sophisticated and central to their economies, cultures and values.

It meant that although the Crown had, over the century and a half since the Treaty, treated Maori fisheries as a commodity that it could regulate and dispose of as it chose, it was mistaken. The legislation passed that professed to protect Maori fisheries had for the most part failed to do so. As the Crown progressively licensed the system, it had taken away rights to commercial fishing from many Maori, and forced others out of the business. In short, the fisheries belonged to Maori, they hadn't sold it, the Treaty protected it, and still the Government had steadily taken it away from them. Now the quota system threatened to take it *all* from them.

The Tribunal recommended that the Crown recognise the rangatiratanga of Maori over their fisheries guaranteed under the Treaty. Ngai Tahu, Muriwhenua, Tainui and the New Zealand Maori Council went to the High Court for a declaration that the quota system was contrary both to the Treaty and the law. In October 1987, a court injunction prevented the inclusion of fish species in the system on the basis that the full, exclusive and undisturbed fishing rights belonging to Maori in those species would be lost to them.

Negotiations between the Maori parties and the Crown finally resulted – after a couple of failed attempts – in a Maori Fisheries Bill which would give 10 per cent of all quota currently in the system to iwi over four years, along with a payment of $10 million. Despite further Maori objections, a rewritten version became law in 1989.

How would it be administered? The Maori Fisheries Commission was set up to deliver the quota to Maori. Initially it would hold it on behalf of Maori, while it worked out how to distribute it. Seven commissioners were appointed, with Sir Tipene O'Regan as the chairperson, and began working out an allocation scheme. Sound easy? Don't think so. It was a country-wide benefit that had been transferred, so the challenge was to establish how everyone who had an entitlement gets a share.

Of course, while Maori were holding this quota, they had some capacity to do some substantial business. And they did. First they acquired Moana Pacific Limited.

Then, in late 1992, they managed a very substantial deal. The Crown agreed to fund Maori into a 50/50 joint venture with Brierley Investments Ltd to bid for Sealord Products Ltd – New Zealand's biggest fishing company. In return, Maori would declare that all their current and future claims in respect of commercial fishing rights were fully satisfied and discharged. It cost $350 million and gave Maori control of roughly a third of the New Zealand fishing quota. On top of that, Maori would also receive 20 per cent of quota for all species not yet in the quota management system.

Bear in mind, though, we're talking just about commercial fishing rights and interests. Any other fishing rights and interests – namely customary food gathering where it's not for commercial gain – still exist, and the Deed of Settlement says so. They're still protected under the Treaty of Waitangi.

At the time of the Sealord deal, the Commission was renamed the Treaty of Waitangi Fisheries Commission, with wider-ranging powers, an increased membership of thirteen commissioners and a requirement that it be clearly accountable to Maori as well as to the Crown.

The Commission was given the task of working out allocation procedures for the assets, and it had to do so under two separate processes – one to distribute assets already held by the Commission (the 10 per cent of quota plus cash and shares, referred to as 'pre-settlement assets'), and a second for new assets acquired under the full and final settlement (referred to as 'post-settlement assets').

So how long did it take to get the distribution done? Would you believe ten years and counting? The problem was essentially that it was very hard to work out a distribution model when some argued that you should distribute to iwi while others said it should take account of urban Maori. However, in 2003 a resolution emerged in the form of the Maori Fisheries Bill, which promised to bring a resolution to the whole thing. Meanwhile, the Commission itself has roared ahead. Shane Jones:

> We control between 40 and 50 per cent of the fisheries, which is an extraordinary situation. The Maori interests would be the largest exporting bloc in the fishing industry. We have about $1.2 billion worth of exports. But Sealord itself has a turnover of about $700 million and at least $400 million of that is export of NZ-based product. Moana Pacific has about another $100 million, and there's probably about another $100 million lying around in the other companies. In Sealord alone, 2400 jobs.

Which is really the point of the settlements – economic clout has been transferred back to the people who had so much taken from them – with remarkable results, in some cases. Sure, there have been stumbles along the way. Tainui invested some of its settlement money in ventures that came adrift, and had to work hard to get things back on track. The doubters loved that, of course, and talked about an iwi elite lording it with their new money. But as John Tamihere points out, Pakeha know a bit about that too.

> At the drop of a hat, our captains of industry crash Air New Zealand, we're in there with $850 million plus another $150 million in capital overnight. I don't even know who the directors were. If they were Horis, they'd have told us.

Evening things up takes time, it seems, but this was a productive time for the Tribunal. Some decisions, however, haven't had such fruitful outcomes. The Tribunal's interpretation of the Treaty has become a degree or two more contentious, and that's been mirrored in other parts of the political landscape. There have been mutterings, noises of disquiet. And largely because of Don Brash articulating those concerns, it has been open season on the Treaty and its apologists.

CHAPTER ELEVEN: THE PRINCIPLE ISSUE

'Treaty principles? Don't make me laugh. It means whatever they want it to mean.'

IF YOU look at what ACT MP Stephen Franks has been saying in his speeches, you'll see that he's no great fan of the way the Treaty has been interpreted. In fact, he is quite upset about it. Everywhere he looks, he sees the Government and its bureaucrats in thrall to an emperor with no clothes. What are these principles, he asks?

> Great leaps of faith are required to understand how these unknowable principles come to mean a duty on the Crown to actively subsidise and promote Maori broadcasting, or a right for Maori to claim ownership (and naturally royalty entitlements) in respect of plants and bugs which have been in New Zealand for millennia before Maori and which will no doubt be in New Zealand for millennia after we have all passed on.
>
> Last year we had the spectacle of the New Zealand Government solemnly lifting tapu to exorcise evil spirits in our embassies around the world.
>
> The Royal Commission on Genetic Modification rever-

> entially went about New Zealand holding hui. The subject was science so recent and so arcane that few scientists have a confident grasp of it. In truly laughable passages the Commission solemnly recorded the signs and portents of these hui, including a bird flitting from rafter to rafter, as showing special significance. They urged the Government to make all haste in ensuring Maori were put in a position where they could exercise their special guardianship and express their exclusive spirituality in relation to indigenous flora and fauna. Apparently these cultural requirements will be satisfied by conferring modern entitlement to lucrative property ownership.

He's right, to a point. The Treaty's being freighted with responsibilities never intended. People have claimed there are things that it automatically imports when it doesn't. Not a word about them. But that doesn't mean the Treaty doesn't have very significant ramifications, or that its principles are completely unknowable.

We know that there are some bedrock aspects to it: Maori do have guarantees in relation to their lands, forests, fisheries and other taonga. Those things are valuable property rights, they do need to be respected and there is substance to them. And we're not working in completely unknown territory any more. We have some very good and rigorous analysis to draw on which keeps things on track. Not the least of those examples would be the *Principles for Crown Action*.

So when you have to look at an Act and answer the question *What does it mean that I must have regard to the Principles of the Treaty*, you're not up that creek without a paddle. But what if you were to change the way you wrote the legislation and actually said specifically what people *have* to do, rather than simply state that they must follow the Principles of the Treaty. Would that be a good idea? Can't see why not. This is an idea that Matthew Palmer has developed. It looks like a pretty good solution:

The core of my argument is that it is insufficient to simply refer in a piece of legislation to something called the Principles of the Treaty of Waitangi. What you actually need to do is to think about what these principles are, what they mean, in the context of the particular piece of legislation that you've got to hand, and exactly how they apply.

That will generally involve identifying how a piece of legislation or policy affects Maori, Maori interests, and consulting with Maori on that effect and weighing up those effects and seeing whether there are alternative options which have effects which are not as detrimental – if there are detrimental effects. It essentially involves taking an approach to the Treaty of Waitangi which is the same as we take to any other policy issue. We actually get into the issue and analyse it. And I think that putting a simple clause in a piece of legislation just referring generally to the Treaty of Waitangi abdicates that responsibility.

The problem is that to do that is actually not easy because there's a lot of work. You've got to think about it. So it's easier not to. It's easier just to refer to the Principles of the Treaty of Waitangi. But that's not what we do with, for example, budgetary matters. I mean, if there are budgetary implications of a government proposal, Treasury will insist that they are examined and we know what something's going to cost before we implement that proposal. The same, I think, is true of the Treaty of Waitangi. You actually need to know what the implications are. You might then proceed in one way or another, but you need to know what the implications are to begin with.

So part of that approach is about not reducing things but making things concrete and practical and looking at what they really mean in practice, rather than engaging in a sort of abstract academic debate about theoretical concepts in which people just import their own fears and prejudices.

Including judges?

Including judges. And in the end if you just have a generic reference to the Treaty in legislation then it is the judges who have to do that, and the judges who actually have to say what a

> policy means, and I don't think that's their job; that's Parliament's job in the first instance.

He says that legislation is beginning to reflect this approach:

> The Public Health and Disability Act 2000 ... does adopt that model to some extent and I think some of the legislation since then, such as the Local Government legislation, has gone down that route. And it may well be that people don't necessarily agree with what's in each piece of legislation but they know what they're arguing about, you know? They can agree or disagree. They can form a position. If you just have a general clause, people don't know what they're arguing about.

In other words, if you don't write it down now, you can have both parties thinking that it means what they want it to mean and they both acquiesce. Only later do they find they have a fight?

> Yes, or they can imagine things that mean what they fear. Part of this, I think, is about being concrete rather than abstract. If you think about the words in the Treaty debates like 'rangatiratanga', or 'sovereignty', or 'self-determination', or 'kawanatanga', to some extent they're all words which are abstract everywhere in the Treaty debate. It would be beneficial to reduce those issues to on-the-ground issues. Instead of talking about where Maori have sovereignty over a bach or foreshore, okay, what are the uses to which Maori want to put this, why is it important to them? This particular headland or beach, how do they use it and why? And how do other people use it and why, and is there actually a conflict in practice or is it actually something that we can work out – because New Zealanders are actually quite good at working out practical compromises. So I think taking the debate to that practical level is helpful.

And the more often you do that, presumably the more comfort you can offer people by demonstrating that this removes elements of doubt?

> Yes, it's like the Ngai Tahu negotiations. They were significant because they introduced instruments of co-management of natural resources and sites of significance. In the abstract, before the deal was done, there was quite a lot of fear in the South Island about what that was going to mean. But in practice, my perception is that things have worked out, on the ground, with respect to particular localities. And people feel much more comfortable about it. And you can see the same thing in the foreshore debate, where you've got people saying, 'Maori are going to have all the beaches,' or 'The Crown is going to have all the beaches' – people get afraid of that.

A nice solution to a difficult problem, perhaps. But we need to remember that there are other dimensions to consider. The problems Don Brash and Stephen Franks alluded to didn't just arise from words in the statutes. They also arose from operating practice in the bureaucracy. And that's been guided not just by the thinking about Treaty principles, but also by contemporary thinking about biculturalism and the rights of indigenous people. And although those are distinct issues, all those strands have become tangled up in one another.

Have you noticed how businesses everywhere have taken to clamming up to an extraordinary degree when you try to ask them for information – sometimes quite innocuous? Why? The Privacy Act 1993. Well, sometimes that's been the reason. But sometimes it's not had a blind thing to with the Act. Because people think it *might* be relevant, they make the Act the scapegoat. *Not my fault, Privacy Act.* The Treaty of Waitangi has been used and abused in not dissimilar ways. Is it an indigenous people's right? Is it Government social policy? Is it a Treaty right? Sometimes it can logically be all three, but sometimes it isn't. And that's caused confusion.

What the law and constitutional provisions say about the Treaty, and what this legalese is taken to mean in the real world, have come to diverge very considerably – and it's given the Treaty an unfortunate reputation.

CHAPTER TWELVE: THE 'GRAVY TRAIN'

'And when you do get hold of someone to consult, they never turn up.'

THE NICE thing about being a grown-up is that – in theory at least – you get to make your own decisions and choices. No one tells you what to do. But rubbing along with one another, we actually find that sometimes we have different priorities and values, and sometimes they clash. The Resource Management Act 1991 recognises that. If we want to organise the world around us so that everyone is in agreement about where the factories go, and what kind of design we want for our towns and cities, we need to have a system that gives everyone a say. Including Maori.

The Government designed Maori elements into the Act with some specificity. Tribunal decisions like Motunui had made it clear that Maori cultural values ought to be respected, and that there ought to be a good system for identifying them. Better to find out about problems before you actually start work, so that, for example, you don't put a bulldozer through a sacred site.

However, a problem arises. There's a 'greenmail' potential to it, as the newspapers point out, and as Don Brash has been reminding us. We are becoming 'a society that allows people to invent or rediscover beliefs for pecuniary gain', he says.

> This process is becoming deeply corrupt, with some requirements for consultation resulting in substantial payments in a system that looks like nothing other than stand-over tactics.

Not that it excuses it, but the problem is not confined to Maori. Still, it's they who have been getting a good deal of the focus. Michael Cullen mentions the outrage at fees charged for consultation under the RMA for the new Waikato Prison.

> I think when Pakeha react to that, they're right to react. That's not how this was meant to be. It doesn't look like co-operation. It looks like a pretty grubby kind of cash transaction.
>
> ... It's perfectly legitimate that if you go to marae and the consultation is there and hospitality is provided that you present a koha to pay for the cost of that. But ... I know somebody who's in property development, local Maori come into his office and they have consultation and he pays them a thousand bucks or something. I mean that's just fundamentally wrong. That's not what it should be about. And I think, really, if many Maori stood back and thought about it, they're actually demeaning their own status by getting into that cash nexus relationship.

Tom Bennion jokes that it's 'Simon Upton's fault. And Treasury. I mean, all we're seeing here is the working of Treasury's model.' He points out that early on in the RMA everybody suddenly realised that *you were allowed to make side-agreements!*

> The Act is completely silent about the service station that sets up [and] there's only one property next door and their mortgage has just been mysteriously paid off and everybody said 'That's outrageous', and the Court [comes] back and says, 'No it isn't. That's the efficiency of the regime that allows people to trade away their rights.'

> So if I want to set up a housing development next to you ... you can say you want $2000 to take a holiday to Fiji and that's fine. So there's that point that is completely missed. Buying consents – chequebook planning is absolutely how you do stuff under the RMA.

All the same, he thinks the situation is somewhat out of kilter.

> I mean there are certain organisations that basically have taken millions out of this process. You have people doing things like opposing a very large landfill – the taniwha one, very unfortunate. The principle is right: taniwha can hold up a road and basically the thing got pushed out of the road pretty quickly. Iwi stuff can hold up developments significantly and some of the arguments being raised could be seen as pushing the boundaries.
>
> There are a lot of payments to iwi for this ... every local authority and regional council makes regular payments to iwi to look at consents. They have a protocol – like Ngati Raukawa has someone who sits down and gets every resource consent that comes through and has a look and phones the council back and says, no, not worried about that, or heads up we *are* going to be concerned about this one ... So iwi do have input on the planning process and councils do make regular payments. The fact that that system's gone quietly into place has been good. It's the exceptions that make the problem.

He reminds us, though, that the RMA actually works more efficiently than people might think.

> Just remember, 98 per cent of Wellington City Council's resource consents don't get publicly notified – in an Act which says public notification should be the norm not the exception. The Wellington Regional Council publicly notifies and hears about twenty consents a year. Otherwise they quietly go around and talk to all the parties.

Margaret Wilson stresses that the aim of the Act is to give everyone the chance to have their say about what gets developed around them. Do we actually object to that?

> I think to some extent there, in the RMA, people didn't quite know how to fulfil the requirement – a pretty legitimate requirement – of telling people what's going to happen to them as a result of some development or change. Every New Zealander, whether they're Maori, European or whatever, would require that actually. It's really interesting that people want to change that in the RMA.

Ministers closest to this legislation may see a need for some reform but they also caution that Brash will find his stated aim of ridding it of Maori references will be hard to achieve. Those references are bound into the whole way the statute works. More to the point, why would you remove them? To head off greenmail potential the Act can be tightened, but why deny Maori the protection of the things they most value in the process?

There are examples of consultation where things look a little less well conceived. All kinds of good and admirable things have been done by many good and admirable people in the name of honouring Treaty obligations or practising enlightened biculturalism. But enthusiasm can take you to some funny places, and, if you're not careful, you'll end up getting lambasted by Dr Brash. He offers an example:

> I've had an email this week from a guy who works in a Crown Research Institute. He [was] working on energy research [and] he said *I have to consult with iwi before I do it*. Now that made him very angry. He couldn't see any rational reason why he should consult with Maori New Zealanders as opposed to any other New Zealanders.

When I first wrote about this I also encountered scientists less than thrilled with the consultation requirements. Here's one response:

> In my field we make transgenic organisms. The Hazardous Substances and New Organisms Act 1996 applies to our work and ERMA manages our work. Local panels assess planned experiments to determine safety and to ensure the work is done in a responsible, ethical way. Those panels include Maori representatives. Do you have any idea why? Because I don't.
>
> As you might expect, the Maori are uninformed about the work they are assessing, so we ran a day-long seminar to inform them, something we are happy to do for anyone. They still remain relatively uninformed yet we are required to have them at the meetings and to pay for their travel ...
>
> It's not the resolution of inequities that bothers me. I'm as puzzled and disturbed as anyone by the dearth of Maori scientists, and anything that can be done reasonably to resolve those issues should be done ...
>
> There is now an assumption that the opinion of the Maori matters in every issue above and beyond their opinion as humans like the rest of us – that bothers me. In some cases that opinion is enshrined in the bureaucracy (not necessarily in law) and sometimes that position is being abused ...

There are arguments you can make against this, though. For example, you could say that Maori representation on ethics committees promotes consideration of what research means for Maori development and Maori culture in a way which can't happen if they are not present. If it helps develop knowledge and understanding of science in the Maori community, should we complain? Another view I've heard goes like this:

> Researchers need to stop thinking about Maori as people they need to 'consult' with to 'gain consent' and start realising that Maori have a hell of a lot of knowledge about what it means to live here, and that knowledge is at least as important as the stuff we circulate in our European scientific journals.

John Tamihere sees the money in it:

I see this – that there is a huge dollar value going out from the Government in research and development. A number of people were researching us as anthropologists, and we weren't part of the script.

So I was staunch – purchasing decisions are being made about us, by people not of us, researching us, coming up with, I think, the wrong outcomes. So we need to be part of the architecture of a whole range of research. And why shouldn't we be? Particularly if it's going to have major impacts on our health outcomes, education outcomes.

So in these areas, I'd look at the impact and architecture of the survey or the research and say, well, hey, if it's going to have an impact on us, why can't we have a say? What's wrong with that? And it should be as basic as that, I would have thought. Not a right of veto at all, but a right to be engaged with.

Margaret Wilson looks at it from the researcher's point of view:

I know your research will be that much better – in social research I guess – if, in fact, you are sensitive and aware of the people who you're researching and how they respond and how you treat them and what's important to them. And your research will be better informed if you take account of those things; otherwise people won't talk to you, or they'll tell you what they think you want to hear.

But I think it must also be tested against the evidence, and that's of course an obligation on Maori . . . what is the evidence, what is the tikanga and protocol that's involved here that must prevail? And if tikanga can't be shared, then I think there are some real issues in there. Because then there are no reasons for decisions, and reasons for decisions are the essence of our justice system.

If these issues need scrutiny, we should also be thoughtful about it. Consultation is a very good way of getting people involved before there's an argument or a fight. While you're talking, you're not scrapping. But what about another question Brash raises: should Maori have what he sees as some pre-eminent right to be consulted?

> The Local Government Act 2002 requires that local governments should consult with communities AND with iwi. As if iwi are not somehow part of the community. And that engenders all sorts of feelings that there really are two different rules here.

Well, yes, it might engender that feeling. Especially if you bang a loud drum and say *These people get special treatment*, without explaining what that special treatment is, or why it is being given.

Let's recall the thinking behind the Resource Management Act. Tribunal decisions such as Motunui had shown quite clearly that there were aspects of the environment that were very important to Maori. You don't run a sewerage outfall onto their traditional fishing grounds. You don't go developing on top of sacred burial grounds. You should make due allowance for the cultural values of the iwi who signed the Treaty.

Consulting people so that no harm is done means you're putting the proverbial fence at the top of the cliff instead of an ambulance at the bottom. Is that really so terrible? Is there really any reason for us to take offence if someone gets special recognition, that they should be spoken to?

The phone in our household rings just about every night of the week as we sit down to dinner, researchers wanting our opinion on everything from toothpaste to financial services. Actually, I'd be happy if I wasn't consulted so often, thanks very much. But it really doesn't trouble me that it says in an Act of Parliament that my local council should speak to iwi. Maybe if we were all to reflect a little on the value to democracy of having people speaking to one another, of making a point of finding out what particular people think, we might all fret a little less.

TEST YOUR TREATY KNOWLEDGE 9

The Government presently spends about $7.7 billion per year on health. Maori represent 14.7 per cent of the population. What approximate proportion of the health vote do they receive, including special grants for Maori health?

- **A. 16 per cent**
- **B. 19 per cent**
- **C. 24 per cent**
- **D. 28 per cent**
- **E. 36 per cent**

(Answers page 199)

'Would you go to a Maori doctor who got in on a quota?'

WHEN DON BRASH pointed out that Maori were getting preferential treatment, the media went searching for examples. They had to work quite hard to find some evidence.

The *New Zealand Herald* conducted its own polling of 'What's eating Pakeha?' and 'What Maori think'. The paper asked people to name some areas where Maori get special treatment. They mostly struggled to come up with anything past special admission schemes for some tertiary courses.

So let's start there.

There are 8615 registered doctors in New Zealand: 198 of them are Maori and many of them work with Maori health providers. Typically, because there are so few of them, they're overworked.

So the University of Auckland runs the Maori and Pacific Admissions Scheme (MAPAS), which was set up in 1972. It's an affirmative-action programme that aims to increase the number of Maori and Pacific entrants to medical school. Why? Because they need more Maori doctors in the community. Why? Because the Maori health providers need them, because they're short of doctors. There's a demand, and a need, and this is meeting it.

Can they get in on lower grades? Yes. Can they graduate with lesser grades? Empathically not. Sound unfair or unreasonable to you? As Don Brash likes to say, let's be clear: programmes like these are affirmative-action programmes. They're not Treaty of Waitangi issues. You can make an argument that it's an Article III right, but that's not how these policies took shape.

What of Brash's argument that positive discrimination or affirmative action is racially divisive, that all policy should be formulated on the basis of need, not race? Well, we make distinctions based on social-grouping criteria in all kinds of ways: the legal requirements for women are different than for men in some important respects, for children compared with old people, for people who are mentally unstable compared with people who are not. The law makes hundreds of distinctions. Is it really divisive to run policies whose aim is to put one racial group back on an equal footing?

Sir Tipene O'Regan has this to say about affirmative action:

> I believe absolutely that the devices for driving towards social equity should be based on need rather than anything else. The only thing is that Maori should not be excluded. What Maori have a right to be is whatever the going rate of citizenship is; under Article III, they have a right of access to that rate. And that raises the very interesting question: if they're not receiving that rate, what do you do about it?
>
> Now, that leads you ... to positive discrimination, as you do for people who are in wheelchairs and ... children who are illiterate and the elderly – you attack those areas of citizenship deficiency or benefit deficiency. You attack those with some kind of positive discrimination ...
>
> The bogey that somehow a Maori neurosurgeon is less qualified than a Pakeha neurosurgeon because he has a different basis of access to university is an absolute nonsense ... It's fairly

> plain that a Maori person of middle-class income, educational achievements and background can get a quota benefit of access to med school, and that means that someone else with a higher mark might have been excluded. And that gives rise to misery. And I think it's always going to. Because that raises another question: if you want more doctors, you probably have to have a quota system. The question is, do you want them?
>
> If you want male primary-school teachers, you either have to have a quota for them or you won't get them. If you want women lawyers, at least for a long time you had to have some sort of access quotas. And they've used positive discrimination techniques on all sorts of bases. If you don't have it, you don't get the result that you want. Now I happen to dislike them. I go for the need argument. But as a matter of public policy, we have them in all sorts of cases.

Don Brash, on the other hand, sees it this way:

> Large amounts of education and health funding are influenced by the ethnicity of the recipient. National would fund social welfare on the basis of need, not of race. It would continue to support Maori education and health provision because people should have choice.

The *Sunday Star-Times* tested those assertions and found that in 2003 $158 million, or 2 per cent of the health budget, was targeted at Maori needs; $135 million of this went to Maori health providers, whose services are also used by a significant number of non-Maori. Brash says he would continue this to allow for choice, so what remains in contention is $22 million spent by mainstream health providers and targeted at Maori. In education, the *Sunday Star-Times* calculated that the targeted funding was 1.5 per cent of the education budget. Not exactly vast sums.

Affirmative action is based on providing opportunities for people who might be deprived of them otherwise – simple as that. It is presupposed that the need for such schemes disappears when equality is achieved. Their object is only to level the playing field for Maori so they can participate equally in national life. Is that really so unfair?

In the end, it will come down to your own world view. Libertarians and ACT-leaning voters tend not to like affirmative action; socialists and Labour-leaners do. It's up to you, and it's your choice each election. It's just a decision: do you believe we're creating a fairer society by helping people who need it? And if you can readily identify Maori as a group that needs it, would you support targeting them accordingly?

This is a debate that may run a good while yet. Affirmative-action arguments have been getting Americans hot under the collar and, some might argue, around the neck for many years now. But you'll make much more sense of this if you look at it as a social-policy issue. Treating it as a Treaty one just adds a level of complication it really doesn't warrant or need.

CHAPTER FOURTEEN: CULTURE GAP

'Frogs? Tell me this is a joke.'

GEORGE BERNARD SHAW once observed that a newspaper was a journal that seemed unable to discriminate between a bicycle accident and the collapse of civilisation. There you go, I'm blaming the media. Well, only to this extent: there's something about stories like taniwha holding up projects, and jewellery being banned from schools, and kaumatua accompanying frogs on a plane flight that seems to bring out the beat-up instinct in journalists.

And if you're a politician who's found that the *Bloody Treaty Carry-on* plank has developed a good bit of bounce, you pile right on into the row: *Let me through, I'm an outraged politician!*

That's not to say that cases of this kind don't sometimes expose important issues that warrant debate. But sometimes a perfectly valid principle gets trashed because someone has interpreted it in an odd or invalid way. The tail wags the dog. Just because a principle is poorly applied doesn't mean the principle itself is faulty.

So it is with some aspects of biculturalism. Don Brash has an example he likes to mention. Often:

> I think you saw one good example at Marlborough Girls' College with the necklace. In one sense utterly trivial, but people say, 'Wait on, why can some people wear greenstone pendants and bone carvings and I can't wear a necklace around my neck that I've worn for six years because my father or somebody gave it to me?' . . . There's nowhere at all in the Treaty of Waitangi that says [anything] about necklaces or giving one race the right to wear a necklace and not the other.

True enough. But nor does that mean that on the strength of a policy that doesn't seem to have been especially well considered, all practices that give due recognition to Maori are wrong. And nor does it mean that, in general, there is a policy abroad in New Zealand that Maori culture should be protected and respected, but others should not be. The very fact that the story didn't unleash a torrent of 100 others telling of similar 'scandals' suggests this was an exception rather than the rule.

Furthermore, myths tend to build up around the original story. Take the taniwha example. 'Should we allow the supposed home of a taniwha to hold up a roading project?' asks Brash. Apart from the implied cultural sneer – would he talk about the *supposed* resurrection of Jesus? – there's also an implication that we can expect this to happen often. Not so far, though. How many projects have you heard of that have been held up by taniwha, apart from the one in Meremere?

Here's what actually happened. Towards the end of 2002, Transit New Zealand had to stop work on a 100-metre section of an expressway project. The local hapu, Ngati Naho, said they were concerned about the effect the works would have on a taniwha in that immediate area. Okay. Maybe you don't believe in them. Maybe I don't. But I go to church each Sunday for a communion that you may not believe in. There is a tolerance for that belief in our society, and for the spiritual beliefs of other people as well. (Okay, you might say, Jesus doesn't get in the way of motorways. Well, he would if you tried to build a new motorway through half a dozen different sites in Israel, that's for sure.)

Anyway, within one week Transit New Zealand and the iwi had negotiated a solution and work started again. In the process, Transit New Zealand also solved a problem at another site nearby; they would build a steeper embankment at little extra cost to the project. The news release stated: 'This may cost a little more but, as a result, we are able to preserve a site which has both environmental and cultural value.' How much extra? $15,000–$20,000 in a $75 million project. So, minimal delay, small extra cost. Total number of taniwha disruptions impeding development across the nation to date? No doubt we'll be alerted the minute someone finds another.

However, Brash may have a valid point with this:

> Environmental law is turned into a farce by allowing spiritual considerations to be taken into account. Beliefs are being invented for gain; the process is becoming deeply corrupt.

Without question, when it's not a sincerely held belief, but just a rort, it deserves to be exposed. There's an excellent chance the media will do it – they're waiting for your call now at the *Holmes* show. But it's important to not confuse issues on the fringes of cultural sensitivity – the most obviously controversial ones – with the general notion itself. Taking a few examples and using them to suggest that the country is in the grip of Treaty madness denies the daily and rather more mundane reality.

Similarly, some people see government offices and letterheads with Maori names on them and recoil in horror – *We're in the grip of political correctness*, they fret. Really? You'll see multilingual branding from Quebec to Kuala Lumpur where it doesn't seem to be ripping at the fabric of the nation. If Inland Revenue wants to put Te Tari Taake on its envelopes, perhaps it does no more than provide a simple way to become more familiar with the language (not to mention often making more enjoyable reading than the contents of the envelope).

Likewise, if we pay for Maori elders to perform hikitapu ceremonies at New Zealand posts overseas, there are various ways of looking at it. You might be indignant at the expense. But equally you might consider what it means for the film *Whale Rider* to have been publicised with the help of government funds. In both cases, an awareness of a unique culture is being fostered, and an interest created in what happens in New Zealand.

And then there are those frogs. Don Brash asked:

> Should we pay for three kaumatua to accompany frogs from the Waikato to Christchurch so the frogs can be given a powhiri when they arrive?

When you put it like that, it looks like a bridge too far. But then you listen to the other side. These were no ordinary frogs. New Zealand's native frogs are among the world's most primitive; scientists are fascinated by them. They're what frogs looked like 200 million years ago, and they're unique to New Zealand. Losing them, they say, would be a disaster from a biological point of view. The kaumatua were taking forty-nine of them from the King Country to a captive breeding programme at the University of Canterbury. Compare the cost of those three airfares to Christchurch with the public money spent without acrimony on parades where a silver cup was driven in its own car up and down Queen Street.

Of course Don Brash knows these examples are exceptions, so he leans on their symbolism to make his argument. For that to work, however, they need to be symbolic of something bigger, and for the most part we never see it. The nearest you get is the cultural safety debate – now *there's* something that sets a few people off, nursing acquaintances of mine included – and going by some reports, the health sector has been refurbished with wall-to-wall Treaty studies seminars.

Does the perception match the reality? A nursing degree, Ranginui Walker has written, takes 3000 hours to complete. Of that time, 3.5 per cent is spent on cultural safety training. So it doesn't exactly dominate the programme. The rationale is this: a nurse treats many patients from all kinds of cultural backgrounds, which he or she needs to understand. Nurses won't be as flexible and open-minded in dealing with those patients if they don't have an understanding of their own culture, including some knowledge of Maori and Pakeha history and development.

Yes, there are ways and there are ways of presenting that story. Tell Pakeha that they're a bunch of oppressing, thieving scumbags, and they're not going to much care for the story. Tell them that their ancestors did some misguided things, and you'll maybe get a more sympathetic hearing.

To hear some students tell it, they have felt a bit browbeaten. The term 'cultural safety' itself can sound somehow coercive in a PC way, and tends to make some people bristle. Which raises one of the most relevant questions in this: how far *do* you push things to force the majority to learn an awareness of the other's culture?

Much of the Treaty debate is blurred by the overlapping of Treaty, bicultural and indigenous rights issues and rhetoric. All, to some degree, are invoked when people talk about preserving and fostering Maori culture. Which in turn raises further questions: What is Maori culture? How does it differ from the cultural life in New Zealand today? Is it really so very different?

What you find as you explore all of that are other ways of

seeing the world, and other ways of going about your life. Sir Douglas Graham has this to offer:

> Take something like tangis. We tend, when someone croaks, to rush around there and tell the [relatives] how sorry we are. The funeral's a couple of days later, lasts an hour, bury the poor old bloke, and then everyone goes home, leaving the widow grieving for the next month by herself. With Maori you turn up when he dies, everybody rolls up, friends, everyone. He's lying there, everybody talks to the body, it's amazing. And then three or four days later it's all over. You know – which one's best? There's a lot to be said for it.

But finding admirable things in another culture is not the same as enshrining indigenous rights. Doug Graham again:

> I don't have any problem with saying the Maori people have a special status in New Zealand as the indigenous people, in the same way that the First Nation people of Canada or the Aborigines have a special status. They're not the same as everybody. They share all the same rights as everybody else, but they have some others. Okay, now some people find that – and I think Don [Brash] is one of them – a bit difficult, but I don't have a problem with it.
>
> But again, how many Maori people in 2004 are actually as concerned about this? I suspect the vast majority have lost contact with the marae, they're not that fussed about claims really. They know they're not going to get anything out of it personally, nor should they. So they're happy enough just to plod along just as long as they're getting enough so they can pay the bills. But those that do return to the marae and listen to debates between the elders, and the older people and the aunties, they still feel very deeply about the claims. It's important we don't lose those people.

It was with that in mind that state money was allocated to Kohanga Reo and Kura Kaupapa – the immersion kindergartens and schools that have helped revive the Maori language. As have radio and television. To facilitate that, the Waitangi Tribunal had to look at one particular word in the Treaty – 'taonga'. It's been contentious, and you can expect it to remain so. Under Article II, as we've seen, Maori are guaranteed protection of their lands, forests and fisheries – and also of their taonga, or 'treasures'. Vague word that. Tricky. Could it mean airwaves? The Tribunal said yes. Kiwifruit? No.

Where did this come from? Alex Frame points to the trend under Rogernomics towards the wholesale privatising and commodifying of all kinds of property:

> Of course Maori were going to say *Well, we never thought of this as being property before but hell, if it is property, it must be OUR property* … Immediately, those really irritating – for Pakeha – demands that the airwaves were Maori property according to Article II – water, dams, rivers, foreshore, seabed have all emerged out of this climate.

As the Tribunal has ventured into the area of taonga, and also into the question of whether Maori have been unfairly deprived of their rights to oil and gas, and whether the proposed foreshore and seabed policy breached the Treaty, its relationship with the Government has become strained. In three instances now, the Government has said it wouldn't accept the Tribunal's recommendations. Michael Cullen:

> It's supposed to be a fact-finding body. I think the problem with the Tribunal to some extent is the tendency to effectively take assertions by Maori as fact, and there's not a lot of testing of the facts. And that was all right, I think, when you were dealing with historical claims where the broad outlines of the outrage were pretty obvious. So the occasional flourishes around the edges of that weren't too important. When you start getting into issues like oil and gas and all those sorts of things, actually the testing of the facts becomes a lot more important. And that's why I think the Tribunal has been shown up a bit

> more in terms of not being entirely adequate for that role.
>
> ... If successive governments keep rejecting its recommendations in these contemporary areas, it loses credibility ... I mean, that chapter on tikanga is very interesting, but if you read it from a Pakeha perspective it almost seems to say, 'Well, only Maori can know what tikanga is and you're never going to find out, we're not going to tell you, you've got to accept what we tell you it is.' Now that's not a basis on which a rational debate in a bicultural, multicultural society can occur. And that *will* lead to increasing explosions of Pakeha anger which will not be conducive to good society or government.

Margaret Wilson says there's a difference between hearing historical grievances and contemporary ones.

> So it's a set of jurisprudence that's operating really totally outside the mainstream. And there are some real issues about that – if it's not connected solidly to a statutory base, then it's not surprising governments don't really take account of it in terms of recommendations, because it's almost impossible for them to do so.
>
> Courts will not decide hypothetical issues. They will decide a specific dispute on the basis of evidence and according to the rules of evidence. So there are rules around how you do it. And the outcome therefore is enforceable because it's specifically between two parties; there's a body of law, there's an application of evidence.
>
> The Tribunal doesn't work like that ... [it] deals with collectives, for a start. It doesn't deal in an accepted and understandable base for evidence. Therefore, when it frames its decisions, it may not necessarily connect it with something the Government can actually do anything about.

Criticisms of the Tribunal's rigour and status, Wilson says, are valid to a point. But ...

> It's actually deeper than that. I think [the question is] 'What *is* the identity of the Tribunal?'

Now, there are some who want it to be a Court. And by that they mean its decisions are enforceable. If its decisions are to become enforceable, it's not a Commission of Inquiry. It's totally different. And I think that's where the problem has come from, because as a Commission of Inquiry it's there to hear a range of really rather loose evidence. It has quite broad jurisdiction in what it can do. And it makes recommendations on that basis. Many of those reports now are looking more and more like court judgments. And therefore it sits uneasily.

It's a body that only one group appears before, and that is Maori. And it's a grievance-hearing body, but grievance-hearing without contested evidence in many ways. I mean, the Crown does appear and does put argument, but it's hard to know what you're really arguing, because courts work on precedent, and a Commission of Inquiry does not work on precedent. So every time you go into it, you're not quite sure what's going to come out the other end.

So I'm very much supportive of a good think about what is in fact the nature and role of the Tribunal. A lot of time and energy is absorbed in contemporary claims, and contemporary claims that result in recommendations that governments are really constrained in not being able to realise, often, in any meaningful way.

On the other hand, John Tamihere points to an example where the Tribunal's role has dovetailed well with legislative agendas – the contentious area of copyright issues arising from native flora and fauna used in commerce and research. The Government, he says, has been incorporating changes in legislation as the relevant issues have emerged in the hearings.

So if you have a look at our copyright legislation, which has just gone through the House under this Government – patents and all those sorts of things ... in large part, the flora and fauna claim has been satisfied. But it's been satisfied incrementally while the claim's been going.

We can perhaps take two main points from all this. If you like everything the Tribunal has to say, you may be in for some disappointments ahead. But if you're worried that Don Brash is right, and the Treaty locomotive (let's not say gravy train) is out of control, you can probably relax a little. The Government has shown that it won't accept just any interpretation of the Treaty that's put to it. There are some pretty clear boundaries being maintained around the Treaty definitions.

Which still leaves us with one major concern raised by Don Brash – that the Treaty is being used to afford Maori a higher form of citizenship than other New Zealanders – to which we must now turn.

CHAPTER FIFTEEN: THE CO-OP SOLUTION

'If we don't put a stop to this they'll end up running the whole show.'

ALTHOUGH WE don't have civics classes in our schools as they do in America, we do all prize this principle of democracy: *one person, one vote*. We don't much like the idea of the numbers being stacked. So when Don Brash says, 'The Treaty of Waitangi must not be a basis for giving greater civil, political or democratic rights to any ethnic group; the present Government is doing that,' he tends to get a good hearing: *Can't have that.*

If it were true, he'd have a good case, but it's the same problem again. When you look at what's actually happening, you begin to see that this is a case of crying 'Fire' when someone's only lit a cigarette. To take the specific example of local government, Brash has asserted that:

> In local government, Maori wards are undemocratic, and special consultation with Maori gives iwi veto power over many job-creating development projects. National would remove these features.

If that seems like tilting the table, then what do we think of rural wards for councils? They make it possible for small communities with special needs and concerns to get an assured representation that isn't crowded out by the bigger votes across the whole voting area. Should we have a go at them as well for being undemocratic?

You might be wondering about Environment Bay of Plenty. That's the regional council that asked the Government to pass legislation to set up Maori representation on the Council based on the Maori electoral roll. Why did they do that? Well, take a look at these national voting statistics. In 1992 only 2.5 per cent of people elected to local councils were Maori. In 1995 it was up to 3.5 per cent and in 1998, 6 per cent. In 2001 it was back to 4 per cent. The voice isn't there.

Environment Bay of Plenty saw a problem in that. They thought there ought to be Maori members giving the Council some guidance when it was obliged to consider Maori culture and values under the Resource Management Act. This legislation wasn't forced on them by the Government; they asked for it. It's not compulsory – a council can choose whether or not to use it. In other words, people weren't voting Maori onto the Council. The Council – which *had* been voted on – wanted to have Maori working with them. They asked for legislation to make that possible. People's democratic rights are hardly threatened by that.

What about this claim of Maori veto power that Brash raises? Well, that's really confusing the right to be consulted with the right to turn a proposal down. The body that makes the decisions is the one it always has been under the RMA. When you make a resource consent application to build that extension to your house, it's the consent authority – your local council, for example – that makes the decision in the first instance. Then, if you're turned down and want to appeal, it's the

Environment Court. But it's not Maori. If they don't like what you're doing, they have to persuade the authority with a satisfactory case. That's not veto power; that's the democratic process.

Now, Brash may argue that the possibility for a little quiet greenmail behind the scenes amounts to a veto power. If that's so, surely the solution is to change the way the Act works in order to bring those practices out into the light. But doing away with the right to be consulted would be just plain undemocratic. You don't want to throw the baby out with the bath water.

These problems stem from those uncertain Treaty interpretations: the power Maori signed away under Article I of the Treaty – kawanatanga – versus the power they retained under Article II – tino rangatiratanga. Over the past decade or so, we've seen various efforts in various government bodies to make room for Maori, in line with the idea of recognising Maori rights to a seat at the board table. Sometimes it has looked like tokenism – just plonk a Maori in as advisor – but these days some organisations are getting to grips with doing it properly. Moana Maniapoto offers an example:

> My experience is that putting one Maori on a board of non-Maori to represent all Maori views does not work. But if you have got a strong policy, a brief, like we have with the tobacco control strategy, and you have got a body to advocate it, then you're parallel and you have got something to work with. Otherwise you get some poor Maori stuck on a board, that's meant to be the be-all and end-all of everything Maori and they have got no policy to [advocate]. They are just going on their feeling and anecdotal stuff . . .
>
> I was on the smoke-free coalition, just one Maori voice, but nothing tangible to advocate on behalf of, no evidence-based research. When we finally got our policy, our priorities were different from the Pakeha coalition. Bit of a bummer . . . So we

> had a few teething problems, a bit of tension there between opposing priorities. But it's all worked out. In the end, we got our cessation programmes and the Pakeha agencies have acknowledged that that was right and correct and they are very proud of the success.

But she sees a possible retreat being beaten as the debate picks up:

> One of the fallouts for me is that – and it is a direct fallout, I believe, of what Brash has done – I tried to use the health model to form a Maori music industry coalition ... to develop it economically ... with a whole lot of keen Maori music players, producers, artists and that, and look at identifying a set of priorities to move the Maori music industry along.
>
> ... So we talked to all the various ministers involved and the Prime Minister and Judith Tizard and they were all very supportive. So we started this thing up, and we went on the music export development group, which [Jim] Anderton started up and ... it was really choice.
>
> ... And so we were well on the road to being able to work within the industry and we'd formed all these relationships and all that – and Brash comes out and all that potential source of funding dried up. Just like that.
>
> ... It's easy, everyone loves music, it's glamorous, it's not hard ... and that's what we were after. We didn't want just a nice let's-all-feel-good-about-NZ-music, but we actually want to see Maori musicians make money and be economically successful with their studios and all that. But I doubt that's going to happen now.

This is largely a question of power-sharing, and Alex Frame points out that if you look at the Treaty relationship as one of co-operation rather than partnership, it becomes much easier to work out how to share that power:

> It's not that the Maori voice is going to be half. In some matters, such as the future of language, the Maori role is going to be

> determinate. So it cuts both ways. However, in the deciding of national issues, such as matters like immigration, nuclear policy and so on, democracy must run its course. To dangle some illusion that this can be one race, one vote is not only dangerous but it is in a sense a cruel deception. Because it couldn't possibly be so.
>
> I think my starting point is always going to be co-operation ... Government can say we want to work with Maori. Let's talk specifics, let's not have a mechanical model. If it's to be health, if it's to be education, let's sit down, let's look at the problems we face. Sometimes it may involve Maori managing some things. Sometimes it might be a question of shared management, sometimes it might be a question of consultation, and sometimes it might be a question of approaching matters in a global way ...

There are already examples of this idea in practice. Maori education, from preschool through to tertiary levels, is making huge advances. In health, there are now over seventy iwi and Maori organisations funded specifically to provide mental health services. Child and family services that place children who need care and protection with members of the whanau are also growing. Some of these services end up dealing with the most difficult cases, the ones that mainstream providers can't cope with.

Moana Maniapoto gives the example of smoking programmes, which she's been closely involved in:

> Maori have got a right to be healthy, like everybody else ...We have still got one in every two adult Maori smoking. And that's despite quite a bit of effort being put in during the last five years. But that hasn't changed. It makes perfect sense that Maori develop our own programmes and strategies to try and combat that because previous ones developed by non-Maori haven't worked for Maori.
>
> But I know that many programmes developed by Maori will

> work for Pakeha. There is a little programme called the Aukati Kai Paipa programme – they've got thirty-five sites around the country – which has got one of the highest international quitting rates in the world. And it's a really collective approach to quitting. People working with their own families. Treating not just the individual, but the family. That's a model that can work anywhere. It's not just in line with the Treaty obligations, but it just makes common sense, economic sense.

Another example: tertiary education institutions. You'll find their mission statements referring to the Treaty, but what does that mean practically? It means things like ensuring that Maori are involved in decision-making, that there is regular consultation with Maori, that Treaty policies are understood and that they're working properly; that there are courses on Treaty awareness being provided for staff, that there is support for Maori staff and students; that they offer courses dealing with Maori aspects of knowledge and culture and so on.

None of this has to be intimidating or difficult. It's just a question of making a proper place for the indigenous culture in the running of the institution. A generation or so ago, we were seeing a lot of the same changes being made for women. Today, those changes are familiar and accepted, but they didn't come quickly, easily, or without a lot of resistance.

You can have a debate about whether the Treaty actually contemplates all of this, but with or without it, you'd be having this debate anyway. There's a movement worldwide for indigenous people to have their place duly recognised in societies, some of which you find enshrined in international law. Even with a treaty that may or may not require it, you'll still quite likely end up needing policies to achieve that.

Which is not to say that they can't end up being implemented in a ham-fisted or unfortunate way – and that's where a lot of the friction can arise. But running into trouble is no reason for giving up and taking back all the power. Planning a future is a task for both parties to a treaty.

TEST YOUR TREATY KNOWLEDGE 10

Last year, the Court of Appeal gave a decision which gave rise to the current debate about ownership of the foreshore. What did that case decide?

- **A. Maori own all the beaches in New Zealand.**
- **B. Maori can take full ownership of a beach if they can prove they used to fish there.**
- **C. The foreshore and seabeds in the Marlborough Sounds belong to the local iwi.**
- **D. If you ask the Maori Land Court to decide whether you own a piece of foreshore and seabed, they are legally able to make a decision.**
- **E. Parts of the coastal land in the Marlborough Sounds belong to the original occupiers.**

(Answers page 199)

CHAPTER SIXTEEN: LINES IN THE SAND

'Not one grain of sand more.'

THE GREAT problem about the foreshore and seabed issue is that unless it gets sorted out, Maori will own every beach in New Zealand.

Right? Actually, no. Nothing like it.

The problem with this whole debate is that it's been based on what people have *imagined* might happen rather than what has actually happened. Think back to the late 1980s for a moment, and recall the gloom and mild hysteria surrounding land claims. As we've seen, the sky didn't fall in. Settlements were achieved, people weren't turned out of their homes, and the country wasn't bankrupted. The whole thing has turned out to be quite manageable.

That's not to say that this isn't a tricky issue, and one that has been brewing for some time.

You need to go back to the beginning of the 1990s. The marine farming industry in the Marlborough Sounds was really taking off and water space was running out quickly. Marlborough iwi – eight different ones – were worried about the impact of all this growth on their customary fishing rights.

They were applying for resource consents to get into the industry themselves, and failing every time. They were objecting to consents for farms that threatened their own customary rights, and failing every time. If they couldn't get any joy under the RMA, they thought, was there anything else they could do?

Well, as it happened, there was. There was a case to be made that they still held customary rights to the foreshore and seabed in that area.

Let's get a definition of that, before we go any further. We're not talking about the whole beach – just the part of it that gets wet. Foreshore is the part between the high-water mark and the low-water mark. Seabed is the area on the seaward side of the low-water mark.

Now, what do we mean by customary rights? Here we need to think about sources of law. The Treaty of Waitangi is one source of litigation. People can go to court and say you've breached the Treaty of Waitangi, but they can only do that where the Treaty is referred to in a piece of legislation.

Then there's another source, very long established. That's common law, which is law made by judges over the centuries, in England and in other Commonwealth jurisdictions like Australia and Canada.

And there's one more source to think about: law about aboriginal and customary rights. That's essentially an element of English property law, which holds that people who are indigenous to an area have an interest in that area and in certain uses of the resources – the doctrine of aboriginal title.

Now, when the iwi took their claims to the foreshore and seabed to court, they weren't arguing about their rights under the Treaty. They weren't asking the Maori Land Court to recognise their claims for recognition of customary rights. They weren't claiming that the Crown has taken away their rights to the foreshore and seabed; they were maintaining that those rights still exist and should be recognised.

For a long time the Crown assumed it owned the whole of the foreshore and seabed (apart from a few areas in private ownership). But that assumption was turned on its head when the Court of Appeal delivered its ruling in 2003. The result was that Maori could take claims to the foreshore and seabed to the Maori Land Court, and see if they could prove they had a customary right, for which the Maori Land Court could issue a title – far from a foregone conclusion, as Matthew Palmer explains:

> The Court of Appeal judgment gave a number of different hints in it that in the end they may find [a case for customary title] quite hard to make. But they also said, 'But you can have a go,' in that court, in that particular area.
>
> Have a go. See if you can determine that you have customary rights or aboriginal title in that particular area of beach. It may be quite hard for the following reasons but have a go anyway. The Court said, 'We're not saying you can't have a go.'
>
> The unfortunate thing to my mind was that the Government then said, 'This is potentially really significant, we're going to do something about this.' It *was* significant, but the way in which the debate took off from there inflamed everything – it polarised opinion. And suddenly you had a number of Maori interests thinking actually the Court had found the foreshore and seabed was theirs, and you had a number of non-Maori interests thinking the same thing and not liking it, and the whole tension was raised.
>
> ... If the reaction to that decision had been, 'Well, okay, the Court said you could have a go, have a go, we'll oppose you in the Court, but let's see what the Court says,' then at least after that Court's judgment came out ... then you would at least have known what you were talking about and you'd be able to come up with a view about that particular piece of land, and how to use it. So I think it's an illustration of the dangers of generalising too much and abstracting too much.

Michael Cullen, however, says the reaction of some Maori worried the Government.

> [They] saw the capacity, if you like, to transfer the Maori concept of ownership into the Pakeha concept and thereby gain almost a huge windfall out of the Court of Appeal decision. That's why the Government, right from the beginning, said: 'Can't go there.' And while we got a lot of criticism for the immediate reaction, there's a lot of looking back here. The way the answer boards lit up on talkback radio immediately the decision came out, you couldn't have been mucking around for very long without getting one simple message out there: 'No, there is not going to be new private ownership.'

So what did the Government do? They went out and said exactly that, in pretty emphatic terms: no new private ownership. And they started working on legislation to make it so. *We'll change the law so that you can't go to the Maori Land Court, prove that your customary rights exist and get a title issued to that piece of foreshore and seabed. We'll frame it so that Pakeha aren't worried about their access to the beach, and we'll make sure that Maori still have their customary rights, and everyone's happy,* they thought.

'Yeah,' as the saying goes, 'right.' Start talking about access to beaches and people imagine the worst, as Michael Cullen describes it:

> I think the fears most of all were that you won't be able to go to the beach as of right, or if you went, Maori were going to charge you to get on it, doing a kind of a clip-the-ticket exercise, which Maori said they never would do. But it was also clear, I might say, that in a lot of discussions in this office there was a general claim to control developmental rights, with potential large cash consequences.
>
> On the other side, I think, the sort of irrational hope . . . was that what the Court of Appeal's decision meant was that Maori owned the foreshore and seabed – full stop – as full beneficial owners. Well, that's not what [the Court] said.

The Government put together a discussion document, and took it to a series of hui around the country. *Not best pleased* would be a polite description of the reception they got. Michael Cullen describes the feelings he encountered:

> The one thing that was said in all those hui which I think was the most perceptive comment was actually from Nanaia [Mahuta's] mother – Dame Te Ata's sister – who said that what was really the problem here was the Maori concept of ownership versus the Pakeha concept of ownership; that the two were in head-on conflict. And I still think that's right. And really what we're trying to do is recognise as best we can within a contemporary context the Maori concept of ownership, while providing legally for the Pakeha concept of ownership.

The arguments went on. And in due course the Government proposed to legislate that the foreshore and seabed be vested in the Crown. Maori, who might have been able to prove they had customary rights over certain areas, and who might then have been able to get a title from the Maori Land Court, were now shut off from that option. Instead, they would be allowed a collection of other entitlements to safeguard those customary rights.

What the Crown gets: full legal and beneficial ownership of the foreshore and seabed. It has to be held in perpetuity, and the only way a government could ever sell it would be by passing an Act of Parliament. *All* the foreshore and seabed areas around New Zealand? No. Only the area that isn't already covered by private titles registered – or being registered – under the Land Transfer Act 1952.

So if you're Maori, you're having all those rights taken away? No. There are a number of provisions to recognise the rights you might otherwise have had.

Firstly, the Maori Land Court will be able to recognise your ancestral connection to particular areas of the foreshore and seabed. You may also be able to strike an agreement with the Government about an ancestral connection under, say, a Treaty of Waitangi settlement, or in a case where you hold customary or freehold land abutting the foreshore. What's the point of it? Well, the Government argues that if you have the connection recognised, you'll have a recognised say in any of the decision-making to do with that coastal area.

Secondly, if you have customary rights in the foreshore and seabed, they can be recognised by the Maori Land Court and the High Court, although it won't apply to areas in private title. How will you qualify? You'll have to be applying on behalf of an established and identifiable group; you'll have to be able to show that your activity, use or practice has been integral to the culture of your group and that you've been using it more or less continuously since 1840 and still are.

If, as a matter of law, the right has already been extinguished, this won't bring it back to life. The Resource Management Act will be amended to protect your customary rights. In broad terms, it gives your customary rights a high priority in consent hearings, and excuses you from a number of the requirements that the Act would otherwise impose on you.

Thirdly, you can go to the High Court and get it to declare that if it hadn't been for the Crown passing this legislation, the bundle of rights you held would have been enough to get you a full territorial customary right over an area of the foreshore and seabed. You can also go directly to the Government to get that recognised, if you choose.

What will this mean to the ordinary New Zealander? Michael Cullen:

> They see that fundamentally this doesn't affect how they go about their ordinary life. It will give more substance and

> protection to specific customary rights. It will give Maori the chance for their day in court, and it gives certainty around the legal status in terms of ownership and beneficial ownership, which I think the Court of Appeal direction left a bit, sort of, muddy.

Well, maybe. But if you were driving over the Auckland Harbour Bridge late in April, you'd have noticed a few thousand New Zealanders who weren't so sure it was such a good deal.

A hikoi was making its way to Wellington to protest the proposed legislation, and there was a good deal of anger at what some saw as a betrayal. There was a feeling that the Maori Land Court, which had power to grant title, was losing that right – not because it was the right thing to do, but because nervous Pakeha had to be reassured.

When push came to shove, the feeling was: *You guys are taking the other side. This may be our property, and you're taking it away from us, again.*

Pita Sharples issued a news release saying that:

> The legislation extinguishes rights long protected in both the Treaty of Waitangi and the common law and replaces it with a newly invented set of 'customary territorial rights' that are effectively meaningless. The legislation has unfortunate similarities with nineteenth-century confiscation laws and is equally unjust.

On the other hand, although you'll hear Maori say, 'We own the foreshore and seabed,' no court has actually yet said so. This could be a protest about losing the chance to get something that might not have been gained.

And there was a groundswell of Pakeha objection and supposition that implied little faith in Maori, who had been saying very clearly that, whatever happened, they would continue to allow all New Zealanders to have access to the foreshore and seabed.

Matthew Palmer acknowledges that it's hard to get this right:

> ... The Government is clearly wanting to reassure the non-Maori public that they will be able to access the beaches. And that's actually quite an important cultural value for New Zealanders generally, I think.
>
> The difficulty they're going to have with the legislation is whether they say ... that the implication of that is that Maori rights, aboriginal rights, aboriginal title rights or customary rights are extinguished. Because in order for a court to find that is so, Parliament will have to say so in almost those words, very explicitly. And that, I think, will be another political problem.
>
> So it's a very difficult set of issues for government to deal with. It's also very easy for opposition parties to make political capital out of. But if those opposition parties ever think they're actually going to be in government themselves they'd be well advised not to, because they're going to have to find a way out of it in the future if they ever get into government.

This is, if you'll excuse the expression, a fluid issue. But something that historian Michael King had to say about this in an interview last year bears repeating. He thought the problem would be resolved in a satisfactory way. And he argued that what the Government was offering Maori was more than had ever been offered before, and 'a hell of a lot more' than they would get from National, ACT or New Zealand First. His thinking seemed to be that Maori had been 'blinded' by the spectacle of the Government siding with the Pakeha constituency, but that calmer heads might come to see the value of what was actually being offered.

We'll have to wait and see.

CHAPTER SEVENTEEN: THE GOOD NEWS

'You give them the money, they just waste it and then come back for more.'

ON A morning just before Easter 2004, I went out at dawn to Hoani Waititi marae in West Auckland. I'd been invited by a friend to the blessing of their new school. *Come and see what they're doing*, she'd said, *it's amazing*. She was right. A place like this would fill the hardest heart with optimism.

Everywhere you look, you'll find opportunities for learning, all the way from Kohanga Reo – the language nests for pre-schoolers, on through Kura Kaupapa Maori – the primary school organised around Maori principles and all taught in Maori, a Wharekura – the same thing at high-school level, and on to employment-training courses. There are 'kaumatua flats' as well – housing for elders subsidised by the marae.

If you've been thinking *This culture and identity thing is just so much flannel*, you need to come and stand in a place like this and see what it does to bring people together and give them a sense of purpose and belonging. It's a bridge back to a culture and identity for young Maori who've grown up not speaking the language, and out of touch with their roots, but that's only part of the picture. A place like this provides support and motivation and opportunity. It has the capacity to turn lives around.

The morning of the blessing, we walked through new classrooms filled with art and posters and instruments and books and photos and writing and projects, and you could feel the pride and excitement of the hundreds of people there. In the speeches kaumatua spoke about the promise for the future that this held – helping the children learn the language, the places that would lead them, and the unbroken chain that bound them. They talked about the new Maori TV channel that had just opened and how so many of the Kohanga kids from this marae were the people now making those programmes, sharing the language and the culture and the stories. Pita Sharples, who has been a guiding force at the marae, was galvanising as he talked about the promise of the future.

There is a real sense of purpose at this marae. There's a place and a role for everyone. If something needs doing, it just happens. There's a spirit of working together and getting things done. They know the power of collaboration, which of course was the driving force behind the success that iwi were enjoying in those early years after the signing of the Treaty.

They do more than teaching here, though. I spoke with some of the people who are dealing with kids in trouble. They'll take them in and try to put them back on track, possibly through training, possibly through the marae-based justice system – whatever might work as a solution. One of those involved in that part of the work had this to say about the Treaty's role. Settlements, he said, were a good way to get some restoration of the asset base and that would help generate momentum for some iwi:

> But here in West Auckland we need to do something about the kids who are in trouble in dysfunctional families. They're in their early teens, and they want to get out and away from that, but there's nowhere for them to go. That's the kind of help we need.

It's that old problem – the cycle that needs to be broken. The marae can make an enormous difference, but it can't do every part of the job.

Which brings us back around to government policies. When Maori began the great drift to the cities, it wasn't to take up highly skilled jobs. Shane Jones talks about an apparent expectation that they would fill the blue-collar jobs and be 'hewers of wood and carriers of water', which, as we've seen, is how things turned out initially. Then the jobs got fewer, and life got worse for many Maori. But over the last generation things have begun to change for the better, and many of those changes have sprung from the kind of policies that are now being questioned and criticised.

Let's look at what's happened over thirty years of opening up opportunities and levelling out the playing field. The very first thing we have to face is that the statistics today are by no means as good as you'd want them to be. But don't underestimate how much improvement has been made over the course of one generation: gains in education, in jobs, in health, and in the Maori economy.

Shane Jones' blue-collar jobs are slowly changing too, as greater numbers of Maori get into education younger and stay in it longer. We're seeing more graduates, more trained people going into a wider range of jobs than ever before – health, television, tourism, scientific research, music, fisheries, forestry – and in far corners of the world, as Moana Maniapoto points out:

> I'm just doing this resource for an organisation – a diary, a bilingual diary – and what we decided to do was put on every page a profile of a Maori achiever in different areas, like sports and art, just a couple of lines ... What I found really fascinating, just doing that little bit of research, was that people are doing things all around the world that we don't even know about. Top javelin, fencing, just amazing things, inventors – and it's not just rugby and league and music. I found 300 or so. Fascinating things and I think we need to remind ourselves of that.
>
> We had a *celebrating Maori women judges* [function] at the Governor-General's the other day, which was really nice. It was straight after the Brash thing and everyone thought, *Jesus, we need to feel good about ourselves*. There were, I think, six Maori women judges. There's lots of positive things going on out there and we don't really hear about them.

The driving force for this is education, and the starting point for a growing number of young Maori is the Kohanga Reo. There are 700 around the country and they're having a big impact on lifting the rate of Maori getting a preschool education. There are now fifty-nine Kura Kaupapa, and four of them are secondary schools. In 1971, three-quarters of Maori were leaving school with no qualification. By 2002 that had dropped to just over one in three. Seventeen per cent of Maori aged fifteen and over were enrolled in tertiary education last year. In 1999 the figure was 10 per cent.

All of this inevitably leads to better job numbers, and a greater proportion of Maori working in skilled and professional jobs than there were a generation ago. Maori unemployment is now down to 10 per cent from a high of 25 per cent in 1992.

As well as that, Maori business is growing and diversifying. Maori now control between 40 and 50 per cent of the fisheries, with the largest exporting bloc in the fishing industry: $1.2 billion in exports and 2400 jobs in Sealord alone. The Treaty settlements have made it possible for big iwi corporations to become major players. Tainui, after a shaky start losing $54 million in investments, has been able to restore itself to $171 million – around the level at the time of the settlement. Ngai Tahu has been building from the beginning; its 2003 annual report showed a rise in total equity from $276.6 million to $300.4 million over the year.

Moana Maniapoto recalls that Ngai Tahu's approach didn't immediately win them respect:

> I know that Ngai Tahu used to be regarded a little bit dismissively, prior to their settlement and I know when [the settlement came out] everyone goes *Oh, you will be using that to help sick Maoris get better and prop up the school and bring back the language and all that.* And they appeared to be building up their company assets and being very corporate and a whole bunch of us are going *Oh, what a bunch of … what a Pakeha response.*
>
> But now I think that they are taken really seriously as a force to be reckoned with, as having really good business sense. Now they appear to be setting up their scholarships and they have got their relationships with the university, and in hindsight it's like they made some really good decisions. And now people don't look at them in the same way. *Gee you were quiet, but boy were you guys onto it!*

The small businesses are growing too. Work Trusts are being established by redundant workers up and down the country and finding new markets and setting up jobs and training. New businesses are being set up in a wide range of areas – from fishing and tourism to aquaculture, high-tech businesses through to fashion. A lot of those businesses are exporting. When you add the wealth produced by existing incorporations, trusts, trust boards and small business, the Maori economy comes to $4.3 billion.

Wondering how that compares with all the benefits and

welfare payments? Try these numbers: Maori households receive $2.3 billion in that form, but the Maori economy pays out more than that in tax: $2.4 billion.

So what is all this growth doing for jobs? Maori employment has actually been growing – at times faster than that for Pakeha. That's not to say that there isn't still a long way to go. Maori unemployment is around 10 per cent, overall unemployment is around 4 per cent. But the solution for Maori is to be picking up more skills and spending more time in education, and the numbers tell us that graph's going in the right direction.

At the same time, there's been another very important factor at work: the Maori cultural renaissance. We've seen a revival across a wide sweep – carving, art, music, preservation of traditional arts, kapa haka competitions. Maori are involved in all kinds of creative work – writing, film and TV production, and music. It's creative, it's dynamic, it's innovative and it's bringing a whole culture and identity to life again.

Moana Maniapoto is one musician who has played a large part in this. What does she make of the cultural revival and the role it plays?

> All those kids that are on Maori TV fronting the news are all Kohanga kids. It's just fantastic. Other nations look at us for the iwi radio network that's been set up. [It's had its flaws] but it has been really powerful in terms of providing a forum for debate and speaking and talkback and things like that. And it's only because we never got it in the mainstream system. If it was all sorted there, there would have been no need for that. But it wasn't sorted.
>
> I've seen rappers in Germany, and I think *Gee, how come these guys aren't winning Grammies*? They are just everywhere. And it's not until you go overseas that you realise, you do need a point of difference. Even if you're not using that, even if it's not a marketing ploy, like I do it; I sing in Maori because I love it and it makes me feel good and it seems to make other people feel

> good. But if you're going to be cynical little record company marketing people, I'd be getting you to do some things in Maori.
>
> I went to a church in Detroit, a Baptist church, and me and my Uncle Syd and his wife were the only non-Blacks in there and people got up and did prayers and sang and carried on and it was like being at the Apollo Theatre. That was when I had my little epiphany. Because what they did was they asked me to get up and sing. They said *We've got a Maori-Indian sister here and she's a singer* and so they asked me to get up and sing. And you know, I had previously really wanted to be Black and sing, and then at that moment, surrounded by 600 Blacks who all sounded like Aretha Franklin, I thought *Jesus, now's a good time to be really Maori.*
>
> So I sung a Hirini Melbourne song and did a few actions and they were blown away. That's when I sort of clicked as a musician that what was right in front of my face was very valuable in terms of my professional career. We just always take it for granted. It's always here ... What's exciting about Maori culture at the moment is that a lot of what we've taken for granted we're realising can be really useful in lots of ways. You know, that collective approach, the traditional ways of doing things, language and all that stuff.

She talks about children she's seen who haven't had a lot to do with marae except on school trips, who aren't sure how to behave properly on a marae:

> They mightn't be able to understand what that means to them, but they certainly do understand that they are Maori and they are viewed as such. And I think that the kapa haka competition is ... a real example of how young people are clear on their identity, their pride.

So how does she see the Treaty fitting into all of this? What effect has it had?

> I would imagine that Kohanga Reo and Kura and the various health programmes, Te Mangai Paho with all its hairy bits, the

> iwi network, and all that, those are all built on Treaty obligations. Funding has been got through that avenue, hasn't it? If we didn't have that, Jesus, I don't know where we would be.
>
> I think that it would go a long way to actually calming everything down, for people to know *what the Treaty means* in a real sense. Well, for a lot of Maori, it's that they have spent a lot of time and effort mortgaging their houses to be part of a claim. It means for others that they can actually go to a whitebaiting ground that their grandparents went to and get their quota. It means for others that they work in setting up educational units attached to the university where they can teach their tribal stuff and revive their language and history.
>
> … I think that if you ask people, even Maori, *How does the Treaty impact on your life*?, for a lot of people their first response will be *Oh, it doesn't a lot*. But they actually don't realise how it's so tied up with everything now. It's just about choice really, at the end of the day … Something we never had when we grew up.
>
> We've run these workshops – a couple with Pakeha too – and everybody once they learn, they go *Oh, that's why you guys are going so nutty, that's why. Now we get it. Now what do we do?* It's not a Maori–Pakeha thing, it's not a black–white thing, it's a justice thing. And I think New Zealanders have got a really good sense of justice. They know the facts and then they're cool. But it's all the distortion that's really unhelpful and divisive.

That negative subtext to the Treaty debate – *You're wasting your time, whatever you give them they just waste it* – ignores the evidence of the economic and cultural renaissance, most of which you can attribute to government policy designed to right Treaty wrongs and get a derailed culture back on track. That culture has responded. It's not to say that there isn't still a poverty cycle to be broken in many Maori homes, or that there aren't a lot of social statistics still to be corrected. But in one generation the graphs show that a tide has turned. Logically, as long as the policies that made that tide turn are maintained, the recovery should gather pace.

Sir Tipene O'Regan sees an implicit assumption in the race-relations discourse that those who wish to identify as Maori are somehow backward-looking, that they should somehow be dressed in 1840s clothes. The majority culture, however, is assumed to be culturally superior.

> Somehow or other the majority culture is the source of all new technology, all ideas, all innovation, all change. They fancy themselves the source of it, although they don't feel any debt to China, Japan, anywhere else. Somehow they feel themselves synonymous with all the brilliant innovations of Switzerland, America, the West. Somehow it's all the gift of some Scousy migrant on Auckland radio talkback. He actually feels that he brought it all to the natives. And this comes through in discussion continually.

Of course, that's fundamentally wrong. And as a new generation of Maori once again show how adaptable and energetic and determined they are, that way of thinking is going to be confronted with more and more evidence to the contrary.

TEST YOUR TREATY KNOWLEDGE 11

If the Government passes a law that declares who owns the foreshore, who can fully and finally overrule them?

A. The Supreme Court
B. The Privy Council
C. A large enough group of registered voters
D. The One News team
E. The Waitangi Tribunal

(Answers page 199)

CHAPTER EIGHTEEN: CONCLUSION

'One law for all New Zealanders.'

WE LIVE in an age of sound bites, talking points, and simple political slogans. If you want to win an election campaign, you need to make your message as concise and punchy as possible. You may have only seconds to make your pitch before the bored TV viewer reaches for the remote, or clicks their mouse to another website. What's a poor politician to do? Well, here's one thing you can do: take a tricky issue that really gets people's backs up, and tell them there's a nice simple solution to it.

One law for all New Zealanders has a nice ring to it, don't you think? The trouble is, a nice simple solution is really just a new jar of snake oil if it won't actually work.

Our history tells us that we have a problem today because of one that began 150 years ago. Two parties signed an agreement to work with one another to share this corner of the world. The hope was that both parties would benefit from what the other had to offer. But one party welshed on the deal. The settlers got what they wanted – land – and failed to deliver what Maori though they would get – an active role in the growing economy.

Instead, their economic base – their land – was gone, and

they had to make their way with little to support them. Late in the piece, but not too late for it not to work, successive governments have taken steps to put Maori back on the footing they otherwise would have had. Settlements and new policies have had significant results. The culture has come back from the brink, and today it's flourishing.

You can attribute the recovery to several strands of government policy – belated recognition of the Treaty, a worldwide trend towards recognising the rights of indigenous people, and the social policy that all welfare states have practised over the past hundred years or so. You can also attribute some of the tangle we have – and the mess that so vexes Don Brash – to the mingling of those strands.

Brash says we can fix some of this by taking all Treaty references out of legislation. The trouble is, it could be one of those solutions that create more problems than they would cure. Michael Cullen takes issue with the interpretation the policy implies:

> What Brash is really saying is there are no contemporary expectations which are legitimate under the Treaty, and he's really saying that the Treaty is just a historical document and if we nicked land off the Maori in the nineteeth-century then that's awful and we should sort of pay a bit more over to compensate for that, but beyond that it has no real relevance today.
>
> Now I think that's profoundly wrong and will be profoundly divisive. It will shut up talkback land for a while, until the reaction starts occurring. And as I said … when Brash and I debate [this]: 'Well, you may think you can say that you'll take all the Treaty references out of the legislation, but the lawyers and the judges will quickly collude to put it all back in again through case law. Don't think this will stop this stuff happening. It certainly won't.'
>
> So with a huge Maori renaissance you're going to say, 'Sorry,

> we don't really like any of it, and you're going to be just New Zealanders, full stop'? It's a non-deliverable, as business people like to say.

An alternative solution – such as that suggested by Matthew Palmer – might be more workable. The problem, he says, lies in the vagueness of legislation drafted to 'have regard to the Principles of the Treaty of Waitangi'. The inherent uncertainties are left to the Courts to work out. But if you look carefully at the legislation being drafted, you can ask specific questions: *What are the Treaty issues that come up here? How do we address them specifically, and what rules and requirements should be in here?* That gets you down to a manageable, specific level, where common sense can prevail. Everyone can have their say, debate the specifics and hammer out an agreement about what should be in the legislation:

> In Canada, in the United States and Australia, the same issues arise. They come up under different legal headings in the US and Canada: they talk about aboriginal title. And they have negotiations, they have settlements of aboriginal title claims, rather than Treaty claims, and they talk about self-government. The same underlying dynamics are there in terms of the relationships. The same is true here, which means that if we didn't have a Treaty of Waitangi, the same issues would come up under some heading or other, whether it be aboriginal title, customary rights or something else.
>
> Similarly, I think that if one branch of government fails to deal with the issues then another one will have to. Now, I actually think that it's better for Parliament to deal with these issues because you've got more direct democratic influence, and these are essentially policy issues which Parliament is equipped to consider. But if Parliament doesn't deal with them and they don't get considered properly in legislation, then you will find the Courts having to deal with them, and if Parliament doesn't, for example, spell out what it thinks

> the Treaty means, the Courts will have to do it in a particular context.
>
> And at a constitutional level, if Parliament keeps avoiding what the constitutional place of the Treaty is, then the Courts may well at some point feel that in the interests of clarifying our constitutional arrangements, they will have to declare what its constitutional place is.
>
> ... So it's not that the Court would say that Parliament can override the Treaty. But it may be that a court – and I could quite easily see a court saying this in the right circumstances – would be prepared to say, if Parliament's going to act inconsistently with the Treaty, given everything it's said and everything the Crown said, they need to do so explicitly.
>
> The implication of that is you'll either have a whole lot of legislation saying this abrogates the Treaty of Waitangi, which is going to be a problem, or you're going to have a whole lot of legislation that doesn't say that, in which case the Treaty is superior to it. So I think it would be in Parliament's interest to work out this question before the Courts get to that.

So, to remove Treaty references from all legislation would effectively also remove the main mechanism for the two parties to resolve differences and disputes?

> I think so, because if you're Maori and you have a problem with government policy, then at the moment you can go to court, in quite a lot of areas, and say, 'You're not complying with the Treaty ... you need to consult with us.' ... If that goes then what do you do? You probably take direct protest action, and I think that is likely not to be as healthy as dialogue.

Of course, removing Treaty references is not the sum total of Brash's prescription. He also asserts that there should be one law for all – no preferences, no allowances on the basis of race – and he claims that current policy is divisive.

Margaret Wilson takes issue with this one-size-fits-all approach, which she characterises as 'Everyone has to be like me in all aspects of life.'

> It's actually quite rigid, and I'd say that many European New Zealanders don't subscribe to that either ... It's a very authoritarian, and if I might say, quite a simplistic notion of it.
>
> I don't know why people are so afraid of difference, because it's essentially part of who we are and that's why, I think, if you actually analyse what Don Brash and [others] are saying it is a denial of history and [the] reality of how people organise themselves.

Sir Tipene O'Regan sees history repeating itself in the *one law to rule them all* idea:

> The most extraordinary thing in the Brash Orewa speech is ... It's all there in the nineteenth-century Hansard. Same argument. The principal arguments advanced in the New Zealand Settlements Act for the dispossession of Maori of their assets was one law for all. Rights and privileges of British citizens. One law for all. It's a whole assimilation urge. And the fascinating thing is they don't really mean it.

Okay. Let's say we don't follow the *one law for all* path, but we still want to get things a little clearer than they are now. Would a Commission of Inquiry help? Sir Douglas Graham wonders if it would get off the ground, and wonders, if it does, what it's going to do:

> It might actually do more harm than good, in a funny sort of a way. A lot of these things you're just better to get on with it. And sometimes, the less people know the better, you know, realistically.

Perhaps, then, you're better off to let sleeping dogs lie. Trouble is, they're all barking madly at the moment. If we want to work out how we mesh together social policy, rights of indigenous people, the Treaty, and – as the foreshore debate has shown us – aboriginal title, we probably need to take a systematic and comprehensive look at the whole thing. A Commission would be no bad way to work that out. Handled well, it could well come up with a lot of fresh thinking about the place of the Treaty in our lives. Moana Maniapoto:

> We need to encourage visionary, pioneering creativity that might lead to fundamental change to establish a new set-up that will operate within the Treaty relationship.
>
> I think there is far more synergy between Maori and Pakeha, especially those feeling the brunt of government policies, but politicians and the media historically tend to scapegoat Maori for every ill.

In fact, she argues, Pakeha have a lot to be thankful for because Maori have a history of consistently challenging the status quo and leading attacks on globalisation and all its practices:

> We have a history of creating models that inspire other peoples around the world and there is no reason why those models won't work for non-Maori here in New Zealand.

She also thinks there should be a full and frank discussion about tino rangatiratanga, and what that means:

> It's at the very essence of the debate and no one from the Crown is prepared to even engage at that level.

Sir Tipene thinks you should be rearticulating the Treaty over time as our circumstances change:

> What about the other immigrants who are coming in who are not part of the Maori/Pakeha bicultural bloc? You've got to have some sort of articulation of that because the Treaty contemplated the arrival of new people. You wouldn't have had it if it didn't contemplate that.

Anne Salmond has been considering some of the issues that flow from that. Could it be that as our society evolves, the old bicultural way of looking at this whole issue is being overtaken?

> There is increasingly a consumer attitude to culture among New Zealanders – you can go to your little boutique culture and pick some bits out of that and you go to the next one and take bits out of that and then play with the combinations. You can see that in many art forms in New Zealand at the moment. There is a great deal of experimentation going on. It's more serious than consumerist, but the artists are certainly doing things which don't fit a binary model.

She points out that in New Zealand, many people have very diverse whakapapa, and the way they assert their identity won't necessarily follow any conventional model:

> When I think, for example, about my students at university, many of them have complex genealogies – you talk to them, and they'll say, 'I'm a little bit Jewish, a bit German, a bit Samoan, and I'm a little bit European' and they want to be all of these things and feel good about it. They don't want to have to split themselves in half or into the various fragments to fit a purist cultural model.

Salmond sees cultures borrowing from one another and responding to changing circumstances. As they come in contact with some other tradition, the bits they like, they take. Maori and Pakeha have done so over the last couple of hundred years, she argues, very actively:

> This idea of pure culture is mythological, and possibly quite dangerous. Like pure race, pure culture – this idea that you have a pure essence which remains intact over time and has to be protected at all costs. Well, we know what happened in the history of Europe with that kind of idea. Often the outcomes are not very pretty.

She wonders if current interpretations of the Treaty that see ours as a kind of binary society split down the middle – with Maori people on one side and Pakeha people on the other – do justice to the heritage of the Treaty.

> We have had 200 years of swapping with each other – genes, language – and so by now, the binary model is fictional. And possibly quite perilous. I support the Treaty settlements because major grievances arise from the fact that the promises made in the Treaty were not honoured. It was signed by the Crown; those were serious promises. The honour of the Crown has always been at stake in the Treaty. But it also allows for whakapapa to join. People get married and end up with a foot in both camps – that should be a basis on which we go forward together, rather than seeing the Treaty as an instrument which cuts us in half as a nation.

She says that the Treaty lays down some ways of working amongst ourselves as New Zealanders that can be applied to everyone:

> The model of good relationships, dealing with each other in a way which is mutually respectful, honouring the traditions of both sides, accepting that they have done a lot of exchanging in the last couple of hundred years, that's a great way to go forward.

Maybe this is a better way of looking at the issues than the binary Crown/Maori model. Salmond offers the example of art and culture and the way ideas are blending and cross-pollinating; people coming together, going to school together, their kids meeting and marrying and having babies together. It adds up to a new reality, she says, in places like Auckland:

> That's going to be the seedbed, I think, of a new vision of the country. I'm not quite sure exactly what it's going to look like. But the mingling is positive, it's great. Tikanga Maori is at the heart of it, but not in a binary relationship.

Being less legalistic and programmatic in our thinking about the Treaty, says Salmond, would help. She sees us wrestling with two competing models, neither of which is actually going to work – the idea of two peoples working together according to the terms of the Treaty, and the 'one law for all New Zealanders' view that would have any differences in treatment determined solely on the basis of need.

The problem with the first model, Salmond argues, is that it doesn't fit. One solution might be to draft legislation, as Matthew Palmer suggests, with a greater degree of specificity, but be guided by those broad ideas of the Treaty as a basis for good working relationships between peoples. You would do what was necessary to maintain the wellbeing of the indigenous culture, but you'd aim to do it in a way that reflected the mixing and blending of the cultures that's going on.

Wherever this debate takes us, we know that the Treaty matters a great deal to many Maori. As Michael Cullen reminds us, it was all they had to hang on to for a long time when everything went the wrong way for them:

> They placed their faith in a legal process trying to achieve some kind of outcome and then we rip all of that away – and that's the thing about the foreshore and seabed which still makes me feel a bit queasy. I mean, we are sort of, to some extent, pulling the mat out when a victory has been gained.
>
> Now, I can intellectually and morally justify it, I think, but let's not pretend there's not an issue there. *Of course* there is an issue there. And now to say, 'Well, sorry, having done all that, we're now going to say this is irrelevant just when it's starting to mean something and you're starting to see some gains out of it' – what do we expect the Maori reaction to be to that?
>
> It's going to be one of deep resentment and deep anger in response. Is that good for us all? No, it's not. It's bad for us all if that happens.

Doug Graham says he's not pessimistic about the direction the debate's taken lately:

> We're a great little country and we'll work our way through it. You get people shouting at each end a bit, but by and large most New Zealanders are pretty fair and they can size something up. As I said … no one's trying to do Maori down. I've never met anybody who's trying to screw them. But they do expect them to stand on their own feet a bit and get on with things. And I do too.

Would he see the Treaty becoming less significant over time?

> Well, I don't worry about it being a living document, but Don [Brash] seems to think it's difficult. And I'm not too worried about the principles in the Treaty either, because none of them are terribly earth-shattering. But it shouldn't be regarded as some sort of panacea for everything. That's what it's come to be. You know: *I've got rights here, my rights under the Treaty – passports*! I mean it's all nonsense.
>
> Pita Sharples was on the radio one day recently and … he was quite angry. And then he rattled off what Maori wanted. None of it was outrageous and I really couldn't see why he was so angry. He said Maori fundamentally want to be recognised as Maori in their own country. Why shouldn't they? But nobody thinks about it in that sense. They think 'We're all New Zealanders.' Now to a Maori that means: *Oh, I've got to be sort of pseudo-white. I don't want to be pseudo-white, I'm a Maori.* Whereas we say: *Oh no, that's not what we meant at all. It means you can be Maori all right, but we're all New Zealanders.* So it's just looking at it from two different angles.

John Tamihere thinks we don't give ourselves credit for what we've accomplished in such a short time:

> If you look at [Tony] Blair, his ancestors are 100 years down the road with the Irish – still working on it and blood and guts all over the place. And so if you start to look around the world, this melting pot here is doing extraordinarily well.
>
> I go to a school and because of stereotype they give me a powhiri. But the school is 95 per cent Pakeha. There are only a

> few Maori kids, but the kapa haka group is rockin' – and it's all Pakeha kids … And they're going to be the new generation of Kiwis that will be shaping our opinion about ourselves in the next ten, fifteen years … We just need to ensure that we get through to conclude unfinished business.
>
> The biggest problem I've got with the Brash attack is that in little old Brashville, they just don't have that base information, you know – Doug [Graham] and them got away on them for over a decade – simple as that. So we can help them catch up, that's not a problem. [Some of them won't catch up but] we've got some bloody drongos in our outfit too, you know. Like, Harawira's not going to move. She's in a time warp. This nation doesn't like that, whether it's middle Maori or middle Pakeha, we don't like that nonsense on the extremes. You know, it's pretty good that they're polarising the debate because most of us want to be in the middle of it, we don't want to be on the extremes.

One way to avoid the extremes is to maintain a sense of proportion. Let's consider what we've seen in this story. Are settlements costing us a fortune? Hardly. Is the settlement process out of control? No. How substantial are the preferential rights Maori are alleged to get? Pretty slight, actually. We've made some good progress. Giving more voice to Maori and sharing more power has brought about some impressive changes. Maori business, Maori culture, Maori language, are all much stronger than they were one and two decades ago. The renaissance has given many Maori a new sense of purpose and possibility and they're taking advantage of it. Why would we want to undermine that?

When you look at Ngai Tahu nearly doubling the value of their Treaty settlement in just a few years, do you feel excited about that or not? When you see greater numbers of Maori students in the tertiary system than ever before, do you feel *more* or *less* confident about the future? When you see a flourishing Maori culture in our schools, and kids engaged by it and more motivated to learn, do you see that as a good or bad thing? Wouldn't you like to see more of that?

In the last radio interview historian Michel King gave, he was asked about the division created in the wake of Don Brash's Orewa speech. He said he thought you couldn't measure the seriousness of the problem by the intensity of the rhetoric:

> It's less than a decade ago when there was a huge argument going on over the National Government's fiscal envelope proposal, when they were saying they would restrict Waitangi Treaty settlements to a total of a billion dollars. That caused an uproar at hui up and down the country. It caused Sir Charles Bennett to say that he would advise Maori not to fight for New Zealand again. And yes, it was one of those issues that was talked through and eventually laid to rest, as I'm sure this one will be.
>
> I see the great continuities in New Zealand history as being decency and common sense, and up until now when we've confronted these things we've been able to talk them through, and I'm sure we will with this issue as well.

You can see that all the more clearly if you put things in a slightly broader context. Sir Tipene O'Regan laments what he sees in New Zealanders as a failure of imagination and a 'total absence of willingness to invest':

> You're never held to account for squandered opportunity. You do get held to account over parking tickets. And underwear. There's a whole lot of things that you can't afford to do in this society. But neither can you afford not to do them. The great problem for Maori is that they're too much like New Zealanders. They don't take those great leaps unless they're in an absolutely desperate situation.

Perhaps it's time for a little more imagination and vision. And perhaps it's time for us all to be a little more sober and a little more considered. When you look back over the story we've covered, you see a pretty clear pattern. People fret about things that might happen, and they assume the worst. And yet that dark day never actually dawns. Much of the anxiety comes from fevered imaginings rather than informed thought.

As I write this, we're seeing the same thing again. The sovereignty flags have been flying outside Parliament, and the war of words is being waged once more. At a moment like this, you can begin to wonder all over again if this could be a problem that's just too hard. But it's not. With only a fraction of the difficulty that many nations have encountered, we have been slowly and steadily finding a way to right a wrong and move on. We've made enormous gains. It's no time to quit.

TEST YOUR TREATY KNOWLEDGE 12

Which of the following is not a treaty which was entered into many years ago?

- A. CER
- B. Treaty of Waitangi
- C. Hague Convention
- D. Genocide Convention
- E. Habeas Corpus

(Answers page 199)

Bibliography

Alves, Dora, *The Maori and the Crown*. Greenwood Press, 1999.

Brookfield, F. M. (Jock), *Waitangi & Indigenous Rights; Revolution, Law and Legitimation*. Auckland University Press, 1999.

Christie, Walter, *Treaty Issues*. Wyvern Press, 1997.

Coates, Ken S. and McHugh, P. G., *Living Relationships, Kokiri Ngatahi, The Treaty of Waitangi in the New Millennium*. Victoria University Press, 1998.

Diamond, Jared, *Guns, Germs and Steel*. Vintage, 1998.

Diamond, Paul, *A Fire in Your Belly*. Huia, 2003.

Frame, Alex, *Grey & Iwikau, A Journey into Custom, Kerei Raua Ko Iwikau, Te Haerenga Me Nga Tikanga*. Victoria University Press, 2002.

Graham, Douglas, *Trick or Treaty?* Institute of Policy Studies, Victoria University of Wellington, 1997.

King, Michael, *Being Pakeha*. Hodder and Stoughton, 1985.

King, Michael, *Penguin History of New Zealand*. Penguin, 2003.

Macdonald, Robert, *The Fifth Wind*. Hodder and Stoughton, 1989.

Ministry for the Environment, 'Consultation with Tangata Whenua', 1991.

Minogue, Kenneth, 'Waitangi, Morality and Reality, New Zealand Business Roundtable', 1998.

Orange, Claudia, *The Treaty of Waitangi*. Allen & Unwin/ Port Nicholson Press, 1987.

Oliver, W. H., *Claims to the Waitangi Tribunal*. Department of Justice Waitangi Tribunal Division and Daphne Brasell Associates Press, 1991.

Palmer, Geoffrey, and Palmer, Matthew, *Bridled Power*. Oxford University Press, 1997.

Sharp, Andrew, *Justice and the Maori*. Oxford University Press, 1990.

Vasil, Raj, *What do the Maori Want? New Maori Political Perspectives*. Random Century, 1990.

Walker, Ranginui, *Ka Whawhai Tonu Matou/Struggle without End*. Penguin, 1990.

TEST YOUR TREATY KNOWLEDGE – QUIZ ANSWERS

1 – B
2 – C
3 – E
4 – A
5 – E
6 – D
7 – D
8 – A
9 – A
10 – D
11 – C
12 – E

BEING PAKEHA NOW

Michael King

Being Pakeha Now is perhaps Michael King's most significant work. The first serious analysis of what it means to be a non-Maori New Zealander, it has made a major contribution to our thinking about who we are, where we've come from, and where we might be going.

While recognising and respecting the place of Maori in New Zealand, King argues that Pakeha too belong inescapably to this country and have no other home. They have become, he suggests, a second indigenous culture, that of Pakeha New Zealanders.

His book is an exciting and controversial journey into the hinterland of the national psyche. With the death of Michael King it is also the closest we will get to a memoir by this major New Zealand historian and biographer.

KA WHAWHAI TONU MATOU
STRUGGLE WITHOUT END

Ranginui Walker

'For 150 years the Maori has struggled . . .'

This book is a new history of Aotearoa, New Zealand, recounted from a Maori perspective. For Dr Ranginui Walker the past 150 years have been an endless struggle by Maori for social justice, equality and self-determination. His book provides a uniquely Maori view, not only of the events of 1990 and the past 150 years but also of the entire period of human settlement – and even beyond to the very origins of the Maori people. It deserves to be read by every Maori and every Pakeha.

The revised and updated version of this best-selling book adds two new chapters on the years after 1990 and the on-going strength of the Maori renaissance.

A SHORT HISTORY OF NEW ZEALAND

Gordon McLauchlan

A lively and entertaining account of the story of New Zealand, from pre-European times to the present day. Gordon McLauchlan has assiduously read New Zealand history, biography and fiction for over fifty years and has set out to provide the general reader with a historical narrative that is personal and colourful – stamped with the authority and affection of a lifetime's deep interest.

Written to appeal to all New Zealanders who want easy access to their history, this book will also appeal to tourists and students.

Illustrated throughout

Includes time-line

A SHORT HISTORY OF NEW ZEALAND

Gordon McLauchlan

Includes timeline